VALUES–LEADER!
MESSAGES FR

Fr Harry Bohan has been a priest in the diocese of Killaloe for over fifty years. A qualified sociologist, he is a pioneer in the areas of rural housing and community development. He established the Céifin Centre in 1998, a think tank for values-led change. One of Ireland's leading social commentators, he has written substantially about Christianity, spirituality and economic development. A hurling enthusiast, he is also former manager of the Clare hurling team.

Brian Callanan is a retired planning officer with Shannon Development. He undertook extensive planning exercises in the use of European structural funds in the mid-west of Ireland in the 1980s and led Ireland's first regional innovation strategy in the 1990s. He also gave expert support to development programmes in new EU member states in eastern Europe and was project manager of several European co-operation projects in regional development.

VALUES
LEADERSHIP
CHANGE
MESSAGES FROM CÉIFIN

Edited by Harry Bohan and Brian Callanan

VERITAS

Published 2014 by
Veritas Publications
7–8 Lower Abbey Street
Dublin 1, Ireland
publications@veritas.ie
www.veritas.ie

ISBN 978 1 84730 571 8
Copyright © the editors and the individual contributors, 2014

10 9 8 7 6 5 4 3 2 1

A catalogue record for this book is available from the British Library.

Cover designed by Barbara Croatto, Veritas Publications
Printed in the Republic of Ireland by SPRINT-print Ltd, Dublin

Veritas books are printed on paper made from the wood pulp of managed forests. For every tree felled, at least one tree is planted, thereby renewing natural resources.

Contents

Céifin Conferences 1998–2009

We Need to Be the Change

Harry Bohan and Brian Callanan

We are living through a time of great upheaval in Irish society. The collapse in global financial markets, the implosion of the banking system, the fallout from the burst in the property markets, and the scandals in the Church and betrayal of trust by its leaders have created turmoil. The systems on which we staked our lives are broken. There has been a historic failure of institutional leadership in political, economic and religious systems: the political system has to do much more; the financial system collapsed; the Church has been shaken to its core by a weakening of its moral authority.

People feel betrayed by big institutions and there is widespread frustration and anger. Confidence in these institutions has been dwindling for some time and leadership has been at a low ebb. There is very little inspiration at spiritual or material levels regarding the future. Sectors are pitted against each other for very scarce resources and social cohesion itself is at risk. In short, there is huge uncertainty and anxiety.

However, we need to be careful not to waste our time and energy by becoming part of the 'blame culture'. This is a time for cleansing. It is a time to dig deep at every level in the search for a way forward into the future. Times of crisis can bring out the best in us. This has happened in the past and it will certainly happen again. The question is: how can we create a new way forward that will produce a more positive and hopeful spirit to meet the challenges facing us? We begin by looking at ourselves. In the memorable words of Gandhi: 'We need to be the change we wish to see in the world.'

In looking at how we can be 'the change', this book draws from the Céifin conferences. The Céifin Centre for Values-Led Change was founded in 1998 to understand the changes taking place in Irish society, identify the values shaping these changes, and promote social, human, family and community values. In essence, the purpose of Céifin was to introduce a focus on values in the Irish policy debate.

In order to achieve this goal, over the following decade the Céifin Centre organised a series of annual conferences addressing key issues facing Ireland: leadership; social issues; the inner self; relationships with others; creation and the creator; the role of the modern economy and commercial values, and the implications these values have on human life; suicide; crime in society; and the role of family and community. The twelve conferences spanned 1998 to 2009, and over eighty papers by national and international experts were presented to almost 4,000 people, capturing national attention.

The Céifin conferences were prophetic, signalling many of the inherent weaknesses embedded in the so-called Celtic Tiger: reliance on property-led growth; short-term policies; neglect of sustained economic values; decline of social capital; loss of long-term visions; and the marginalising of human, social and spiritual values. These critiques are topical again today, and they have a strong resonance in the current commentary about Irish recovery, with calls for a renewed focus on core values, sustained development and real competitiveness.

The significance of all this from a Christian perspective is for both an inner and community spirituality that might form the basis of values-led change. Complementing this were the humanistic themes in the search for values: investment in our humanity; discovering our inner selves; empowerment; and overcoming the crisis in our culture. Here, thus, is the unity of the Christian and the humanist around the two themes of inner and collective potential. But these need to be integrated into public policy via social capital, resourcing individuals, and power and leadership – three themes that form the basis for this book.

Social capital of networks between people covers a massive agenda and provides a vital foundation for other actions. This leads on to resourcing people to be centre-stage in any debate about values. It also creates debate about power and leadership based on equity, quality and vision in a global world. All these bring immense challenges. How do we define them? What do they mean? What are the big issues? Where should the focal points be? How are they to be done?

In conclusion, there is an urgent need for balance between the many dimensions that shape people's lives: the social and economic, the spiritual and material, the human and technological, and the local and global. We propose that, to develop balance into the future, attention must focus on several issues: spirituality, institutions, education, sport, family, community and leadership.

A Note on this Book

While the editors have structured the conference ideas in this introduction and given their own conclusions, the core chapters of *Values–Leadership–Change* are from the conference presentations. The book thus draws exclusively on the published material from the Céifin presenters, and is restricted to this material, offered in structured themes that we believe should inform future Irish policy debates. We are deeply indebted to the Céifin presenters and we are also very grateful to the strong chairpersons Rachael English, Marian Harkin, Michael Kenny, Marie Martin, David McWilliams, Doireann Ní Bhriain, Cathy O'Halloran, John Quinn, who stimulated debate. Of course, the approach here aims to focus our minds on the right questions, not necessarily to give any answers – nobody has the last word and we offer this as a framework and a context, not a set of prescriptions. The opinions expressed are purely those of the presenters as summarised by the editors. Of course, needless to say, any outstanding errors or omissions are entirely the responsibility of the editors.

INTRODUCTION

How to Fill the Vacuum with Values

The twelve Céifin conferences took place in the midst of an extraordinary economic boom. While there were economic benefits arising from this in terms of jobs, houses and lifestyles, we were not sure what kind of society was emerging and what values were shaping that society. We wondered, and so the title of the first conference suggested 'Are We Forgetting Something?' What did this mean for the way we were shaping life for ourselves, as individuals, families and communities? We could buy our way to happiness and contentment. Would our children come to believe this is the norm? There was an obvious need for an informed debate as to the impact of the boom, the values shaping us, who were the winners and what was the 'fallout'.

The Céifin conferences attempted to provide that debate. It had become obvious that if we as a society did not get involved in the debate we would eventually lose the language of values – human and spiritual, moral and ethical, right and wrong. Year after year the interest grew and it became clear that significant and relevant issues for our time were being addressed. The annual Céifin conference drew substantial numbers from a cross section of Irish society of all age groups, and gained significant national attention.

Since then, the boom has gone bust. However, we can still ask the same question: 'Are We Forgetting Something?' But now we ask it in a different way. In this difficult time, we ask if we are forgetting our immense inner resources (human, spiritual, community) and how can we mobilise these resources to nurture and strengthen us?

In essence, the lessons from Céifin are that we need to focus on the twin values of our inner identity and collective potential, drawing from both Christian and humanist traditions. We must integrate these values into the mainstream of public policies.

Significant Steps to be Taken in the Future

One of the most significant themes identified at the conferences is the obvious vacuum period we are living through in terms of values and principles. Over the past twenty years we have been obsessed with the economy – roughly half that time with 'boom' and the rest with 'bust'. So where to from here, and what values will shape our future? Is recovery to be based on more of the same market/ money/material values only, or is there a need for a radical change of direction?

It is evident from the conclusions drawn at our conferences that there are issues other than the economy, important as it might be, that shape the lives of people – people we need to focus on. There is an urgent need for balance between the many dimensions: social and economic; spiritual and material; human and technological; local and global; ethics and a free-for-all.

This collection proposes that, to develop this approach into the future, attention must focus on several issues: spirituality, institutions, education, sport, family, community and leadership.

Spirituality

There is an obvious emphasis in the conference papers on the need for a reawakening of the concept of spirituality – personal, religious and secular. We need to search for a soul for Ireland. The new god became that of GNP and economics, with little focus on ideals and values. It was pointed out a number of times there is little real connection between religion and daily life. This has led to the privatisation of religion and the placing of morality and moral values very much in the private/individualistic sphere.

The Christian vision has the potential to provide a basis for values-led change. In the case of the Catholic Church – an institution whose values are based on the gospels, the word of God and social teaching–there is certainly the potential to promote real-life personal, community, corporate and governance values. Sadly, the Church has neglected its own ethical and moral guidelines in the public sphere. As a result, its position is seriously weakened and discredited because of such a breach of trust.

Indeed, all institutions are now faced with a massive challenge to return to their founding ethic.* In the case of the Church it might be important for Christians to remind themselves that Christ asked his followers 'Who do people say I am?' What did he stand for? He stood for truth, trust, integrity and honesty. These are relevant and practical values for our time. So the question 'What does it mean to be a Christian?' must be relevant for us.

> *'The Christian vision has the potential to provide a basis for values-led change'*

The path to recovery must begin with a spiritual, ethical and moral revolution. It is interesting that at a time when our society could be steadily moving away from materialistic values to values that focus on the development of the person, the community and the environment, institutions are moving away from the reality of life for people. In reading the signs of our times, the Céifin conferences highlighted the importance of connecting with people, encouraging and facilitating them.

Concerns about spirituality and its role are not exclusive to the Church, they have implications for the secular and non-religious worlds, with the local and the global, the corporate and public administration systems. Issues of ethics, morality and truth are critical for all dimensions of life. The real challenge for us is how to start looking inside ourselves. We do not need more material growth; the sort of growth we need is inner growth – spiritual

---

* Another example is the banks. They have played a destructive role in Irish society. They spent people's money recklessly and are now cutting personal and community services to regain some of that money for themselves. In doing so, they are cutting the very connections that built trust for them in the past.

growth, on which our culture has turned its back. Speakers at the conferences pointed to the hunger in people, as indicated by the massive growth in literature on the subject of spirituality. A lot of this is taking place outside of organised religion. For example, the nature of practical atheism is that religion is only superficially about God, reduced to the status of opinion.

'The real challenge for us is how to start looking inside ourselves'

Parallel to this is the growth of the influence of the state and bureaucracy, for example the replacement of human beings at the end of phone lines with pre-recorded menus. A curious shift is taking place: as the economy moves more in the direction of private market enterprise, many traditional functions of the home and the community are shifting towards the state.

Unfortunately, as this is happening, what we are witnessing is not a recession but the early stages of a systems failure. We are a culture in confusion because we are the first generation to have reached the limits of what economic and material growth can provide a developed country. It no longer brings increases in levels of well-being across a range of indicators, from mental health to drug abuse to a straightforward breakdown of trust between people. Studies have shown that equality rather than growth is the key to well-being.

We actually know what the future might look like and can describe it. We know it will be based on spiritual well-being, on ethics and morality, servant leadership, balance between the local and the global, on a participative society. But how are we going to get there?

Institutions

The conferences demonstrated that it is one thing to analyse what has gone wrong, but it is another to identify solutions and a way forward. It was stressed over and over again that the freedom our society so badly longed for – from poverty or authoritarianism –

cannot be replaced with a free-for-all. For example, technological development cannot continue to grow at such a rapid pace without an ethical and moral framework – there is a need for values. Values are critical. Inner growth is vital, but at the same time the culture of every single institution that mediates our world – education, religion, health care, financial, business, legal – must be transformed.

To respond to the challenges facing each one, there is a need for ongoing debate, reflection and study in order to better understand the nature of change and ways of adapting to take account of that change. The conferences identified that issues of personal and social development have given way to ones of utility and pragmatism. The dominant influence of technology and economy has led to this, at the expense of human contact and genuine caring. As a result, there is a worrying increase in depression, anxiety and stress. The fact is, a life without people who care may be very rich in many ways but in human terms it is no life at all.

Education

It was pointed out that the world of Irish adolescents changed radically in the closing decades of the twentieth century. Young people, at a time when they should be full of hope, idealism, excitement and expectation, are instead filled with anxiety, as illustrated by the stark statistics on suicide, crime, vandalism and drugs.

What sort of models do we offer our young people – models of responsibility or irresponsibility, value or neglect? We are alarmed at the apparent vacuum in the lives of young people and the manner in which many attempt to fill it. It was pointed out they belong to a society without norms and a culture out of control, with no standards of behaviour, no restraint on its activities. In periods of rapid economic and social change, if traditional norms and standards are undermined and if new ones do not replace them, there is a vacuum. People experience the demise of meaning.

> **'We have become far too smart scientifically to survive much longer without wisdom'**

Where is the solution to be found? Education can obviously play a significant part in helping. The more young people can think things through for themselves, the better. We must encourage our young people to retain a childlike curiosity and a sense of the mysterious. It is said we have become far too smart scientifically to survive much longer without wisdom. A number of speakers stressed the importance of education in exploring the creative talents of young people.

Sport

Sport has the potential to deliver many positive outcomes in terms of quality of life, personal fulfilment, health and well-being. It reminds us that sacrifice, self-belief and teamwork – which are very much part of sport – can help us in life. It also reminds us that sport and indeed living are mere existences without spirit and soul.

Family

The home is the real classroom of life. The family is the place where most learning takes place and so there is a need to give parents every opportunity and support in the vital work of rearing their children. There is a need to place much greater emphasis on family support, including bringing work back into the home through the use of changing technology. Work has always structured the way we live. Looking back to the agricultural economy, everything happened around the home and, in a sense, everyone stayed at home. Then people moved away from the home and went out to work in the factories and the office. People are now spending one or more days working from home. Encouraging this may have economic and social benefits. What is now interesting is the effect this new trend has on the family and on the rearing of children. Children will have some image of what work really means as they see one or other of their parents working. Greater investments in systems and supports for marriage, relationships and family life, with special emphasis on community support, are needed.

Community
Recovery and renewal will come from the ground up. Next to the family, the community is the unit of society that holds people together and supports them. The conferences posed the question: If community values of old were so important, why have so many colluded in its near abandonment? And yet there is every indication of people rediscovering 'community' as the indispensable basis of a sustainable and values-based economy and, by extension, society.

We need to rediscover community and all it implies in terms of a leadership based on service rather than on power, and on respect for the other person, particularly the marginalised. There was a strong suggestion that the failure to understand the importance of community is the single greatest threat to the stability of individual countries and to the stability of the entire world of which we are all part.

> *'We need to rediscover community and all it implies in terms of a leadership based on service'*

An integral part of community is voluntarism. Voluntary organisations do more than provide services. They are about citizenship, belonging and civic expression. They are important building blocks in societal sustainability. The community is crucial for our recovery.

Leadership
To facilitate the growth of these concepts and to ensure growth takes place from the ground up, it is vital that people be given responsibility and participate. For that a new politics is needed: a leadership based on service rather than on power.

The causes of the economic collapse were rooted in failures of political leadership. The causes of the breakdown in the Church were because it disconnected from society and the institution became an end in itself. A radically different kind of leadership is needed for all institutions, with an emphasis on facilitating people to take responsibility. People must be allowed to own what they do.

Trust at all levels must now be earned. Key to this is asking deeper questions about leadership and personal responsibility. We need to build an alternative leadership concept around the idea of service. True leaders have a selfless devotion to public duty. They have a vision and an ability to give practical expression to that vision – a far-reaching vision of the sort of society we want to be when this crisis passes. We need to have courage. We must get back to the truth. We must harness the truth to reflect the change.

We must accept that this type of hierarchical top-down leadership has failed us badly, resulting in the authority of many of our institutions being seriously undermined. If we take out the pillars that we respected in the past, we are left without support. The challenge is now to recreate that support by establishing a different kind of leadership, a servant leadership that will, in turn, empower people to take responsibility for their future.

Finally, a lot of the above will remain wishful thinking unless community by community, institution by institution, voluntary group by voluntary group, political party by political party, we are prepared to identify some of the key steps.

Céifin hopes to initiate this process. There is a real danger right now that institutions involved in drawing plans for the future are doing so without addressing the basics. The very first step that needs to be taken is to consider the founding ethic of the organisation or institution we are part of, and to remember that all change begins in me – my attitude, the way I think, the way I live.

ONE

Value-Led Change

The current economic crisis, and the search for ways out of it, provides the opening questions: What are our collective values? How can they guide us in future directions? This theme was addressed by successive Céifin conferences. But a view shared by almost everybody was that if people wanted a fresh source of values for the future, the Catholic Church was highly unlikely to figure prominently in their minds. For example, **Bishop William Walsh** reported that Jacques Delors, once president of the European Commission, argued the need for a 'soul for Europe', for a deeper meaning and spirituality:

'The hand and glove operation of church and state was often oppressive'

Delors's plea needs to be matched right now with a plea for a 'soul for Ireland'. In our search for a soul for Ireland, we need to look to a renewal of values and principles. Since independence, there have been two dominant institutions in Ireland, the church and the state. In the post-independence years, our politicians were largely idealists who were active in working for the good of the people, with their primary goal of service and principle. The other dominant institution, the Church, was active in support and there was a vitality and a confidence in the Church that inspired so many young people to enter religious life.

There was, however, the darker side. The hand and glove operation of church and state was often oppressive, authoritarian, without accountability and with ill treatment of those who somehow were unable to conform to the strict rules. The 1960s visions of Vatican II, civil rights, change in the world, a new era of dreams were not quite fulfilled. In particular, the inspiration of Vatican II never became a reality. Our Church became too obsessed with what one might call personal holiness. There was a belief that to meet God and attain real holiness one needed to get away from society rather than taking an active role in it. There was little real connection between religion and daily life. This led to the privatisation of religion and placed morality very much in the private individualistic sphere.

The scandals and dramatic loss of confidence associated with the Church, with the loss of confidence in the financial and political systems, has led to serious consequences. There has been a loss of a shared vision and language; we no longer have an agreed way of looking at life. There has been a loss of a sense of moral responsibility, with growing evidence of the privatisation of morality. The new God is GNP and economics, with little focus on the Christian ideals of solidarity. Social capital has weakened and people have become disconnected. Many people have lost a sense of 'interiority', deeper meaning in life, a sense of God.

Looking to the future, church and state must work hard to rebuild the trust that has been lost and take whatever radical action for change is necessary. Ultimately, the church must be at the service of the gospel. The Church has meaning and credibility only insofar as it is at the service of the gospel. The Church and those in leadership in the Church must be motivated by service. Its leadership must be servant leadership rather than privileged or authority leadership.

'Very few of us tell blatant lies, but what of the evasions, exaggerations, self-justifications, the withholding of information?'

If church or state wish to regain the trust of people and to contribute significantly to Ireland in the twenty-first century, we must begin with the truth. We ought never be afraid of truth. Truth can be an elusive creature. Very few of us tell blatant lies, but what of the evasions, exaggerations, self-justifications, the withholding of information? We need to have courage to promote the environment where informed debate can take place about where we are going as a people and what values we want to shape our lives. We need to search for a soul for Ireland.

This call for a 'soul for Ireland' was echoed and re-echoed by numerous conference speakers. Fundamentally, they argued for a reawakening of inner spirituality and personal identity, a deeper resource that had not been tapped by the Church in recent decades. Themes included filling the modern vacuum in values with Christian vision; reimagining our Christian tradition; spirituality of creation; spiritual beings on a human journey; coming back to our own hearts; and the Church as a community of faith. What is significant about all these views is that they point to Christian traditions of inner and community spirituality that could form a basis for values-led change.

This importance of the Christian vision was highlighted by **Fr Peter McVerry** who reported that the vacuum that many people – particularly the young – experience today is a crisis of values.

The Christian vision has the potential to counter these negative values. However, to many people the Church is an irrelevance. Because of poor responses to past abuses, the Church's claim on moral authority has been seriously weakened and the very organisation whose values have the potential to counteract the negative values in society is itself so discredited. The western capitalist economy feeds on consumerism, seeking to persuade us to purchase much and often, and that it is in consuming that our needs can be fulfilled, and that our happiness is proportional to our consumption of goods and services. The related assumption is that our security is to be found in economic terms, and that our security is to be found in our assets and our properties and our bank balances. The capitalist economy also focuses on the individual as the source of innovation and the beneficiary of the rewards of capitalism, thus weakening the bonds and relationships that bind us together.

However, the Christian vision is in direct contradiction to the values of individualism, consumerism and economic security proclaimed by capitalism. Our happiness is to be found, not in accumulating goods, but in letting go of them. Our life itself, our health, our education, our family, our friends, our property, our assets, our jobs, everything is a gift, given freely but given on loan. 'Letting go' is the spirituality that conforms to the essence of our existence as human beings, destined to grow old and die. Life is a giving back to God what God has already given to us. It is in letting go, not in accumulating or holding on, that we find our true happiness and our fulfilment.

How do we actually let go? How do we give back to God what God has already given us? What many *do* find meaningful and fulfilling is giving their energy, giving themselves to make the lives of others a little less miserable, a little more meaningful. It is in giving that both the giver and receiver find meaning. Our security is based only on the infinite and unconditional love of God. Amongst all the gifts we have been given, this is the one gift that is not on loan, the gift given to us at our creation and given for ever.

This love of God for us is mediated through community, through the love of others for us. Hence our true security is only to be found in community. It is in the solidarity with each other in community that we find both fulfilment and security. In building the economic assets of the community, everyone finds security. The assets we accumulate we accumulate not for ourselves alone, but for the community. The spirituality of letting go can only be lived in community, in solidarity with all other human beings.

Fr Michael Drumm continued in this vein about the potential in the Christian vision:

Our economy is in grave difficulty so what should we do now? It is generally accepted in Ireland that we have lost faith in our traditional leaders – in church and state, business and finance. But we need to reimagine leadership, drawing on the riches of our Christian tradition.

We need to rediscover the energy that originally unleashed the Christian vision of the world. The task of leadership is to unleash energy for the future. Our economy and our systems are damaged and in need of healing. Jesus of Nazareth spoke of the reign of God as healing for the sick, hearing for the deaf, new sight for the blind, freedom for prisoners, good news for the poor. Before we can really appreciate the meaning of healing, hearing, new sight, freedom and good news, we need to become aware of the realities of sickness, deafness, blindness, captivity and poverty. When we look honestly at ourselves and those around us, we discover that we are the sick, the deaf, the blind, the captive, the poor, not just in a metaphorical sense but in the physical, psychological, spiritual and economic realities of our lives. Only when we immerse ourselves in these human experiences can we discover who Jesus really was, for his ministry was all about lifting burdens. Whether the burdens were created by selfishness or laziness, a scrupulously strict religious sensibility or blind obedience, political corruption or grinding poverty, sickness or lack of self-esteem, pride or prejudice, the result was the same: people were in need of healing. The meaning of the gospels is not that Jesus was some sort of magician who could solve all of life's most inscrutable problems, but rather that he was one who brought healing and hope into the most abject human situations.

The call of Christian discipleship demands that we always seek to lift the burden. Whether this means helping people to stand up and walk on their own, or exorcising their fear of the unknown, or exploring their minds through education, or feeding them when they are too weak to feed themselves, or opening their eyes to the reality of life, or challenging them to let go of hurts and prejudices, or liberating those who are unjustly oppressed, or introducing them to ever greater horizons of transcendence and beauty, or unsealing their ears to hear the divine echo in their hearts, or unleashing their hope for the future, or sowing the seeds of eternal life. To teach as Christ taught means inviting people to live without the crutch or the grudge or the closed mind.

Reflecting this concern of the spiritual with the real world, **Seán McDonagh** gave the example that environmental damage is a global phenomenon and must be tackled as such by every human being and human institution, especially through spirituality of the Churches.

> *'Human beings and the rest of the planet's community will be condemned to live amid the ruins of the natural world'*

For example, global warming will cause major changes. In northern latitudes, winters will probably be shorter and wetter, summers longer and dryer. Sub-tropical areas might become drier and more arid while tropical ones might become wetter. The changes will have major and unpredictable effects on agriculture and natural ecosystems. As the oceans warm up and expand, sea levels will rise, leading to severe flooding over lowland areas. Unfortunately, the poorest countries, which emit very little greenhouses gasses, will suffer more from climate change.

The Christian Churches must throw all their energies into urgently addressing the challenge of justice, peace and the integrity of creation. Until this awareness is gained in the very near future, human beings and the rest of the planet's community will be condemned to live amid the ruins of the natural world. The Churches must be resolute in their determination to witness to the truth. The World Council of Churches have published a very thorough analysis of the ecological, economic, ethical, theological and pastoral aspect of global warming. All the Christian Churches should throw their moral authority behind this.

McDonagh reported that Dr Chandra Muzaffar has talked about 'moneytheism' as a challenge to monotheism.

Moneytheism is the ideology that legitimises the relentless pursuit of riches as an end in itself as the driving force behind the global economy. This global economy has sanctified the maximisation of profits as a planetary credo. Culture, politics, social life, all reflect, directly or indirectly, the overwhelming power of the ideology of moneytheism. Doctor Muzaffar believes that all the major religions should avoid slipping into pietism or fundamentalism and function instead to critique and challenge this ideology that is creating such cultural dislocation, social injustice and ecological devastation across the globe.

The Churches need to develop a spirituality of creation. There must be a clear appreciation that the *raison d'etre* of creation is not found primarily in its ability to meet human needs. Creation has intrinsic value because it is created by God and sustained by God's spirit, with a strong interdependence of all creatures. We need to have an image of the world as a single cosmic community. Jesus enjoyed an intimacy with nature. In an age of unbridled consumerism, where greed is often represented as a virtue, it is important to remember that Jesus lived lightly on the earth. In this context, creation is understood as a community of beings interconnected with each other and with God. Our way of relating within such an interdependent world must be through communal mechanisms, rather than through dominant or exploitative behaviour.

Reflecting this focus on interdependence, **Michael Rodgers SPS**, founder and director of Tearmann Centre, proposed that the material and the spiritual are one and all things are one with God, the source of life:

> **'Could the call to today's crisis be a call to be more spiritual?'**

We are all spiritual beings on a human journey trying to find our way to the sacred heart of life. The primary place of the sacred is life itself and the universal call to wholeness, goodness, justice, love and peace is heard in the deep heart's core of every single person and is lived out in every detail of life. Our call is to be co-creators with our creative God, participating wholeheartedly in the spiritual unfolding of universal life.

Could the call to today's crisis be a call to be more spiritual? If the spirit is strong, the environment we create around us will be life-giving. It will put us in charge of our own future destiny. How to bring this about is in the hands of every individual and every single community. Spirituality is rooted in the earth where life develops in all its diversity. The road to eternity is emerging in the here and now. We need to become more and more aware of the God of the here and now, and respond to the presence of the divine and eternal in ourselves by trying to be present in everything around us at any given moment.

All of life has come from one source. The universe is alive in itself and has been developing over an incredibly long period of time. It has now reached a stage of such beauty and diversity and complexity that it is almost impossible to believe that there is not a profound wisdom at work in the heart of it. It is the unique privilege of the human to share this wisdom in awareness and consciousness.

There is a crisis looming over all of life on our planet and the main cause of this crisis is human ignorance, greed, exploitation and spiritual poverty. We need to have a heightened awareness of life on this planet. We need to be committed to bringing forth an environmentally sustainable, spiritually fulfilling and socially just human presence on this planet as the guiding principle of our times. Key questions are: Where are we? How did we get here? What is possible for the future? Where do we go from here? We need to look at our economic, political, social and religious situation and how these systems can be changed for the benefit of all people. There is a crisis in the world and we need to be involved with the spiritual, emotional and psychological effect this is having on the souls and spirits of people.

There seems to be a growing culture of alienation and dysfunction in our society. There are few guiding moral principles now and spiritual values have very little influence on human behaviour. There is a spiritual crisis, but the good news is that the human family is well capable of coming up with solutions to solve the problem. We must approach the problems facing us in a positive frame of mind and with determination, commitment and passion. The first step is to believe in ourselves and the contribution we can make. When we come to know ourselves better it is easier to honour who others are and the contribution they have to make too. In spiritual terms, each one of us needs to truly believe that the power for change lies within each person. The challenge then is to become better informed about who we are in the greater scheme of things.

We need to turn away from the limited images of God that we come across every day and turn towards a profound understanding of the God who created the universe and gave each of us a unique part in this unfolding story. As Christians, we must turn towards a more cosmic view of Christ who came to live among us on this earth and blessed our presence here with his example and wisdom, and by his resurrection gave us hope that all things will come to completion in him. It should be possible for us to believe in the Spirit that binds us all together with a bond that is stronger than blood. Maybe the next revolution could be a spiritual revolution. Then the question is how to start planting the new seeds of change that this revolution will require.

Maybe such seeds of change start with the inner person, according to **Sr Thérèse**, Abbess of the Poor Clare Convent, who asked: What has the contemplative to say about this disillusioned society? It was her belief that society is dispirited and disillusioned because by and large we are living 'outside of ourselves'.

Cut off from our true selves, from our own deepest nature, our neighbour and nature itself – disconnected, alienated – and deep loneliness is the result. How well we camouflage this alienation, this loneliness, as we climb the ladder of so-called success. The witness and call of the contemplative life is to 'come back' – to come back to one's heart, one's own deepest centre and 'live' from within there. This was a challenge to you to move into your own hearts, your own deepest centre and live out of there. If you do, then everything will look different. When we do not do that, we are living on the surface, in the control of forces outside of ourselves, and that is not living, that is slavery.

'Move into your own hearts, your own deepest centre and live out of there'

We all have a spiritual or contemplative dimension in our lives and it is precisely because this is so undernourished that everything else falls out of place, resulting in confusion and disillusionment, if not outright chaos. We are so aware of our physical lives and all our glossy magazines tell us in so many ways to care for and pamper the body. But we also have an emotional life and, judging from the increase in marital and family breakdown, it is in a state of chaos. We have an intellectual life as well, but holding them all together at their centre is the life of the Spirit – our 'contemplative dimension' – and this should be an oasis of peace and refreshment because, whether we believe it or not, God is there.

How can I get off this treadmill? How can I get in touch with my deepest centre – my spirit? There is no easy way. Choices have to be made. Do I choose my work to the detriment of my own inner peace, my spouse, my family and quality time spent with them? Can I have time to admire a sunset and say 'thank you, God', or just be with a lonely or elderly person and let them know I care? Choices have to be made. Am I living from within and in control of my life, or am I on the surface, 'outside of myself'?

One thing is certain – our lives cannot have any depth, quality, peace or any measure of real success unless we set aside at least fifteen or twenty minutes a day to be with ourselves and to get in touch with what is going on in our deepest centre – our spirit – to get in touch with God. As great as our need is to get in touch with our inner self, our 'contemplative dimension', is our need to have quality, in-depth conversation to nourish and encourage us on our journey. We could say too what we feed our minds on is what we pray about. What are we feeding our minds on – what is the quality of our reading and how does it influence our lives, our prayer?

Simple suggestions, but incredibly difficult to put into practice. They require great discipline. It is hard to be still, it is hard to go against the tide but it is our sure road back to peace and serenity and our sure way of restoring the balance in society.

Archbishop Diarmuid Martin tried to balance this drive for inner spirituality with the need for organisation. He argued that there is a sort of assumption that whereas an 'authentic' personal religion is very important to people, when people begin to organise religion and establish rules, then the whole thing irks a little. For many, organised religion as opposed to the spirituality of personal experience is somehow less popular, less authentic perhaps – even a distortion of what religion is all about.

'The Church is a communion of communities' Jesus himself would be a little surprised to be told he had founded an 'organisation'. What Jesus left behind was a Church, a communion of communities that meet together to deepen their understanding of the word of God. A communion of communities will certainly have organisational dimensions, but it will have to be defined primarily by its purpose rather than by its sociological framework. It would be foolish, however, to think that a communion of communities, even with only the minimal structure, will not inevitably be tempted to take on organisational structures very like those that are common in the society of the time in which it finds itself. Just as historically Church structures have been influenced by organisational models of different periods, office in the Church has sadly often modelled itself too closely on the authority structures of the secular world.

Contemporary western societies today have an ambivalent relationship with organised religion. On the one hand, there is a rejection of anything that might look like special treatment for the Church which, it is said, should be looked on like any other non-governmental or private body. And yet there is a criticism of organised religion if it fails to take up positions when questions of justice and social concerns are involved.

When we imagine organised religion in the future, we could imagine it more distant from the structures of power, and thus all the more free to influence power. It must become a Church such that those who look at it, even from the inside, will see not a cold institution, but a community of faith that is transparent in its beliefs and practices, a community that worships God, but also a community that witnesses to what God is, namely gratuitous love and a caring and forgiving God. A community that reflects gratuitous love will be an important antidote to a society in which everything is measurable and marketable.

It would be foolish to think that the Church in Ireland has not lost credibility through the recent scandals. Trust and credibility cannot be bought or commanded. They must be earned and when lost they must be earned again from scratch. That earning will be through a renewed witness of integrity. The credibility of the Church of the future will come from the credibility of witness. Transparency will be achieved not just through organisational measures of accountability but above all when the love of Christ transpires as the true hallmark of every institution and organisation that bears the name Church.

The Religious and the Secular: Searching Together for Deeper Meaning

These concerns about spirituality and its role are not exclusive to the Church. The issues raised have implications for the secular world, and linking these Christian issues to the secular dimension is critical, according to **Bishop Donal Murray**:

The secular reality is not alien to the life of the Christian believer and Christians live in the secular dimension. The secular dimension does not need to embrace a particular religious faith in order to make sense. Likewise, not all efforts to grapple with fundamental human questions are necessarily religious. But the secular dimension of life needs to understand the space that the religious dimension of life occupies, to appreciate the importance of questions about ultimate meaning, to realise that it is good for the health of secular society that citizens would be in touch with their own deepest questions. A person's conviction and commitment comes from what he or she believes human beings are and what human life is about. Our quest for meaning comes from reflecting on life's goal. The questions cannot simply be dismissed: Why are we here? Where can we find meaning and fulfilment? With so much evil and suffering in the world, how can we have hope? Not all answers to these questions are religious, but they are at a level deeper than the scientific or pragmatic.

> **'Contemporary culture does not give proper weight to questions of meaning'**

The conflict is not between religion and the secular but between searches for deeper meaning and those who believe that human life has no meaning beyond what can be measured, analysed and scientifically proved. Contemporary culture does not give proper weight to questions of meaning. The result is false conflict between religion and the secular. Religious and secular people can work together on the fundamental questions about the meaning and dignity of life. The religious and secular are like two distinct languages. We need to be bilingual, speaking the language of the beliefs that give energy to our convictions, but speaking also the language of citizenship when we join with our fellow citizens to discuss what is best for society.

This requires a huge effort at renewal, an effort to be in touch with our own deepest recesses, an effort to enter into the thirst of the human heart – first of all our own, and then the hunger and pain, physical, emotional and spiritual, of our fellow human beings, and the longings deep within us for a peace, justice and love greater than anything we know or imagine. Then we have to respond in all the specialised and complex areas of life with the energy and vigour that come from those longings.

The Answer Lies in Our Humanity

Thus, the emergence of secular or humanistic themes in the search for collective values was another strong current in the Céifin conferences: investment in our humanity; discovering our inner selves; empowerment; crisis in our culture; the realm of our unconscious; rethinking our morality; human rights; duality with balance in our lives; linking the local with the global; and understanding our psychological roots.

Then Ireland's Ombudsman and now European Ombudsman **Emily O'Reilly**, speaking at the height of the so-called Celtic Tiger, had much to say of contemporary relevance. She reported that many recoil at the vulgar fest that is modern Ireland: the rampant, unrestrained drunkenness, the brutal, random violence that infects the smallest of our towns and villages, the incontinent use of foul language with no thought to place or company, the fracturing of our community life, the God-like status given to celebrities all too often replaced down the line with a venomous desire to attack and destroy those who were on pedestals the week before, the creation of 'reality' TV, more destructive in its cynical filleting of the worth and wonder of the human soul than anything George Orwell could have imagined.

Is not the speed at which we have jettisoned so much of our religious practice in particular suggestive of a society that was not so much spiritual as spineless, cowed by the power of the Church, observing what we observed out of fear rather than faith? The challenge is how to take and accept this newly secular society and inject it with a value system that takes the best of that which we have jettisoned and discards the worst. It is a challenge equal to that posed by a puzzled commentator scratching his über-liberal head when he observed that he and many like him had spent years attempting to get rid of the hard rocks of fundamental Catholicism from the field that was Ireland. That, he noted, had now been done, yet all that was left was an empty, sterile, barren patch of land. What, he wondered, can we do with it now?

It would be good if we recognised the new religions of sex and drink and shopping for what they are and tiptoed back to the churches. It may not even be necessary to believe, it may be sufficient just to remind ourselves of some of the universal truths about charity and decency and how to live a good life, all of which are contained in the teachings of the major religions. It would be good to regain our sense of the magic of ritual, of the year marked by rites and rituals, not the seamless, joyless blending of undifferentiated weekdays. It would be nice to get the summer over before the Christmas displays begin. It would be good to insert ourselves into the lives of our community, reawaken our sense of what we can contribute, but also what we can receive, the preciousness of belonging, of being caught up in something stronger than your own individual self.

> **'Better life has to do with an awareness of the true meaning of a rich life'**

The answer lies in our humanity – the belief that sometimes people want to do better, be better, and think of people other than themselves. The deeply heartfelt hope that our children will have better lives, and that better life has to do with an awareness of the true meaning of a rich life, of a life where the pleasures of love, of companionship, of reading, of art, of sharing one's gifts, of seeking to attain ever higher understanding of the mysteries, beauties and even ugliness that surround us, are really all that matter.

This need for a deeper understanding was echoed by consultant and author **Peter Russell**, who argued that there is an underlying core to the world's various spiritual traditions:

Spirituality is not so much about spirits or other-worldly phenomena. It is about discovering one's own self, being at peace with one's self in the world, becoming more in touch with a deeper sense of purpose, and freeing the mind from unnecessary fear and anger so that an unconditional love and compassion can emerge. Thus, many of our problems originate from inner human issues. Behind every problem are human decisions, human thinking, human values and human self-centredness. Everything points back to the human being and the human mind. Yet invariably we focus on the problem out there. Whether it is an environmental problem, economic problem, some social problem, or a problem in our personal lives, we tend to look for solutions in the world around us, rather than within ourselves, where the problem originates. We are tending to the symptoms, not the root problem itself.

The real problem lies in the way we think – in our attitudes, our assumptions, and the programmes that run us – what we think is important in life; in other words, our values.

When we look at our values we find that there are several layers to them. On the surface we may value things like possessions, money, social status and the roles we play. But then we need to ask: Why do we value these things? If you look deeper you find that they are important because they give us a sense of security, stimulus, acceptance or attention. But why are these things important to us? What's beneath them? What is it we really want? What is really important to us at a fundamental level? The answer comes down to something very simple. We want to feel at peace with ourselves; we want to be happy. Basically, we are looking to feel okay in ourselves.

> **'This is our true bottom line – how we feel inside'**

This is our true bottom line – how we feel inside. Usually when we talk of the bottom line we mean our material or financial bottom line. But the one thing we all want is to feel happy. We call it different things – inner peace, fulfilment, contentment – but the truth is we want to feel good inside. There is nothing wrong with seeking a more satisfying state of mind. Where we have gone wrong is the ways in which we seek it. We've got locked into a belief that says whether or not you are happy and at peace depends on what you have and what you do. In essence, this belief system says that your internal state of mind depends on your external circumstances. It is this belief that what we have or do determines our inner happiness that drives consumerism. We believe that buying things can make us happy.

The real challenge today is how to start looking inside ourselves, to ask how can we free ourselves? How can we free human consciousness? Until now consciousness was something our culture and science ignored. We know so much about the material world, but we still do not understand how thoughts arise in the mind. There are some who have explored these questions. Mystics, yogies, philosophers examined their own minds. Their quest has been to free the mind, to allow it to be more at peace, and more compassionate. This is probably the most important question that we now need to be asking at this time. How can we free up the human mind?

The answer, it appears, is much simpler than one might expect. The truth is that so much of the suffering and dissatisfaction we experience is self-created. Thus the next frontier for human development is not outer space, but inner space. What we need now is the inner freedom – freedom from outdated beliefs and values – that will allow us to manage our lives and the world around us with wisdom. We do not need more material growth. The sort of growth we need is inner growth – the spiritual growth that our culture has turned its back on.

We need to free the human mind from outdated assumptions and values. Studies in values have shown that people are steadily moving away from materialistic values to values that focus on development of the person and greater responsibility for society and the environment. This needs to be facilitated and encouraged.

However, in spite of this interest in inner space, the growth of secular values has led to 'compartmentalisation' of religion outside mainstream life, raising substantial challenges, according to professor and author **Bill Collins**:

The nature of practical atheism is that religion is only superficially about God, the character of the world and how we should be living in it. In reality, religion has been transformed for the most part into social knowledge, opinion. This phenomenon, practical atheism, parallels the rise of the state. In tandem with the rise of science, the state has become the point of origin for defining the reality of the world and what we should do with respect to it.

As the state has increased in power, its influence has extended to the very way in which we have come to understand our world and our place in it. Religion is therefore to be seen as clearly important to many, but, at the same time, irrelevant. On this reading of the meaning of practical atheism, religion should have little, if any, bearing on the reality of any community-wide problem, and any realistic resolution of such problems must eventually come to terms with practical realities of day-to-day life, which are for the most part ultimately referable, depending on the character and scope of the problem, to the collective resources of the community, that is, the state.

It is likely that practical atheism will intensify and that religion will be reduced to the status of opinion. A secular ethic, oriented to the imperatives of politics and market, will replace the older religious ethic grounded on religion and place. The older way of life will give way and be transformed into a kind of homogeneity supported by a subsidy, increased consumerism and even higher levels of state coercion.

Is there an antidote? There are intellectual tools for resisting the ideological dominance that the state always goes after. The new technology here is revealing that the costs of information have been dramatically reduced and will continue to be so. This is the key to defeating the dynamic of the growth of the state. This empowers the knowledgeable to keep solutions local and avoid the erosion of the natural community order that the growth dynamic of the state can potentially destroy. A population armed with intellectual tools for resisting the ideological demands of the state is in a great position to develop liveable and viable solutions to the issue of practical atheism.

'Empower the knowledgeable to keep solutions local'

This theme of human values was also emphasised by **Paula Downey**, of Downey Youell Associates, who reported that the challenge we face in the world is not so much a financial crisis, but a much deeper crisis at the heart of our culture, our civilisation and the way it is organised:

We need an approach to culture and change based on principles of living systems. In modern times, the pursuit of economic growth has become an unquestioned social goal. In recent years, the annual growth of the world has been equal to the growth achieved in the entire nineteenth century. This has consequences for the breakdown of ecosystems. Twenty per cent of people on earth use up to 80 per cent of the resources, while the rest of the world must make do with what remains.

The irony is that although we have come to believe that economic and material growth are the key to human well-being, the evidence does not support this. Studies have shown that continued economic growth no longer brings real benefits to rich countries, because it no longer brings increases in levels of well-being across a range of indicators from mental and physical health, drug abuse, violence and teenage births, to education, social mobility, trust and community life. In fact, studies have revealed that equality rather than growth is the key to human well-being: in more equal societies outcomes on all these health and social problems are much better, while in unequal societies outcomes are far worse.

What we are witnessing is not a recession, but the early stages of system failure: the collapse of a culture that is based on a dysfunctional story. We are a culture in confusion because we are the first generation to have reached the limits of what economic and material growth can provide a developed country. But we actually know what the future looks like and can describe it in quite some detail. We know it will be based on renewable energy, on diverse transport systems, on the localising of our food systems, new patterns of living and working. It has been articulated in all kinds of places. The question is how are we going to get there? The answer is at the level of the institution. Personal change is crucial. At the same time, our institutions are the forces that mediate our world. Our education systems, transport systems, health care, food systems and other systems are now mediated by institutions that shape our choices and decisions. At the level of every single institution we must effect change: to transform our wider social culture by transforming the culture of the institutions that shape it.

Institutions perceive themselves as separate from the world: but instead they must see themselves as nested within a wider system that they depend on. We need to understand the interdependent nature of reality – systems within systems – and work for interdependency. Institutions have lost their way because they have forgotten their founding ethic: institutions must focus on a purpose that serves life, and does so in an interdependent world. Values are critical: to navigate a path to the future, it is necessary to identify strategic values – simple rules that people can freely interpret in the moment of choice and decision, so that day-to-day behaviour progressively moves us in the direction we want to go. Relationships are key: we must let living systems into organisations so that everyone touched by the system can influence the decisions that affect them. Renewal is central: we must replace planning with learning as a strategy for changing our organisations and learning our way into the future.

'Values are critical to navigate a path to the future'

Linked to these values, the role of the inner person and the challenge to look into our unconscious world was highlighted by Glenstal Abbey monk and author **Mark Patrick Hederman**:

When we talk about the 'dark', the underground, the unconscious, we are using metaphors. The dark, the shadow, the night-time realm of the unconscious, represents the part of ourselves we never reach in broad daylight ... This is the psychological reality, the darkness inside each one of us. We spend much of our lives asleep. This night-time realm of our unconscious is the one that we have to approach and 'climb to'.*

There are a number of ways to 'climb to' the dark of our unconscious. The first way is by being attentive to our dreams. Dreams are the language of our unconscious telling us what we refuse to tell ourselves during our daylight hours. We have to learn to crack the code. Most of us are both afraid and dismissive of the dark side of ourselves. We need to remind ourselves that we carry the dark around with us, that it is an essential part of our make-up, that we never shake it off and move onwards.

Apart from this dream time, there is also the great reminder of this reality contained in the stories of our ancestors. What dreams are to individuals, myths and legends are to peoples. The Irish have one of the great storehouses of such commentaries on our Celtic unconscious, a mythology that is the admiration and envy of other tribes. This storehouse is like an underground labyrinth. European culture, and particularly Irish culture since the foundation of the state, has been constructed over this labyrinth that has been closed off and sealed with impregnable hubcaps, leaving the reality below to fester as in a pressure cooker. These ideals, on which we Europeans base the conduct of our lives, are hybrid and ancient, coming as they do from European philosophy at its deepest and most idiosyncratic.

However, Ireland was kept in the dark about this darkness. Ireland has represented itself to itself and to the world as a light to the nations, missionaries of the angelic nature of humanity, self-sacrificing zealots, both political and religious. We were not the only population to have been consciously sheltered in this

* Paraphrasing W. B. Yeats's 'The Statues'.

way by well-meaning authorities of one kind or another. Our suppression of the darkness and unawareness of the unconscious, our avoidance of all entrances to the underground, were helped by our being an island and the cultural isolation that this made possible.

This produces a schizoid culture that builds itself out of the great divide between spirit and flesh, soul and body, mind and matter, heaven and earth. Such a topography has obsessed the European mind from the beginnings of European philosophy. The way you imagine you are determines the way you decide to behave. The way you decide to behave is your morality. When you believe that the mind is the all-important element in your make-up, then you try to arrange for this one element to govern the rest. In this regard, it has been constantly stated that the head should rule the heart, that reason must govern the passions, that the soul should reign supreme over the body.

But this is despotism. In other words, to trace all that we are back to one or other principle is not simply wrong because it points to the wrong suspect in the identification parade, it is wrong because it seeks to reduce our multi-faceted and variegated network of being to one most basic one. True morality is not about discipline, but about spontaneity. We cannot renounce who we truly are. No morality that forbids us even to enter the attic and examine our proper darkness can be taken seriously in present circumstances.

'True morality is about spontaneity'

This century has been the victim of too many people who were afraid to spring-clean this attic, refused to face the darkness, or dogmatically declared there is no such thing as the unconscious. Art, for example, can provide a door into the dark. However, artists are not enough. Each one of us has to take up the torch and carry on down our own tunnel to the underworld. Our 'proper' dark means what is special to ourselves, and this unconscious is not purely personal, but is shared with others. There is a collective unconscious belonging to particular races that make their darkness more familiar to each other than it would be to an explorer from another tribe. And no tribe, people or nation can absolve itself from this essential task or refuse to make this journey.

This issue of exploration was further emphasised by columnist and author **Peter Abbott**, who spoke of how although the religious establishment has soaked history in blood for too long, the narrative and explanatory power of religious mythology has brought great happiness and succour to millions:

Religious mythology is profoundly effective in helping men and women impose order on otherwise random events. It helps to rescue them from chaos and confusion. Religious myth, however, no longer serves to exercise our moral imagination. Modern Christian thought must bear its own responsibility for smothering the mythical and narrative power of Christianity with orthodoxy and dogma. Perhaps there is a radical way out of this impasse. There needs to be a rethinking of the concepts of morality and ethos that we have grown up with. With the world so apparently 'out of joint', with our moral imaginations being taxed to breaking point, the relatively new synthesis of evolutionary psychology – that branch of science that studies human psychology from a scientific, evolutionary standpoint – may offer a way, at least the startings of a way, out of the mess we find ourselves in.

The task that lies ahead of us involves a rediscovery of connectivity, a continual exploration of the tension between what it means to be an individual and what it means to be a social being, a social being whose society is, increasingly, not just our immediate communities but the whole world.

To inform and direct that exploration requires a new moral framework, tough enough and flexible enough to bend with the winds of globalisation and global turmoil, a moral framework predicated on the organic, life-giving power of the human imagination. It sounds like a big idea, and it is. We can make a difference by helping each other to connect the dots of our individual experiences into a collective and continually evolving experience that could, given nurture and care, transform ourselves and our world.

'A new moral framework giving power to the human imagination'

This emphasis on individual and collective experience leads to a concern for human rights, according to Amnesty International's **Sean Love**:

Human rights are inherent to each and every one of us. They span all areas of life: civil activity, political freedom, social needs, economic well-being, cultural pursuits and environmental quality. Human rights are not just ends or goals to which we vaguely aspire. Nor are they some perfect utopia that we can all dream about. They are the benchmarks of a just society. Moreover, they provide the means to deliver real justice and equality. In essence, they give people the right to have control over their lives and futures. While human rights are the entitlement of everyone on an equal basis, the level of development of a society can be measured by the extent to which we include and protect the most marginalised and the most vulnerable; by our standards of accountability; by the extent to which people are empowered.

Managing these differences and contrasts, and the need to find common ground and balance in the immensity of our experience, is the real challenge, according to poet, philosopher and environmental activist, **John O'Donohue**:

Everywhere the human eye looks, everywhere the human mind turns, there is a huge panorama of diversity – the difference that lives in everything and between everything. The difference that inhabits experience and the world is not raw chaos – it has a certain structure. If you reflect on your own experience, you will see that you are already familiar with duality – light and darkness, beginning and ending and so on.

The really fascinating thing is not that these dualities are there, but the threshold where they actually meet each other. A notion of balance that is really authentic has to work with the notion of threshold, the threshold between light and darkness, soul and body.

> '*All creativity comes out of that spark of opposition where two different things meet*'

Duality is informed by the oppositions that meet at this threshold. All creativity comes out of that spark of opposition where two different things meet. Experience is working all the time with duality, with that energy of opposition within you. The imagination is the faculty that gives the duality within us expression and allows its forms of opposition to engage with each other. For example, there are poor people who have absolutely nothing, but who have a depth of creative imagination that allows them, even in bleak circumstances, to inhabit a gracious, challenging and exciting world.

Another lovely quality of this imagination is its passion for otherness. The experience of otherness registers most firmly in what we find strange or totally different from ourselves. The oppositions that are in us often constellate themselves in terms of contradiction. What is interesting about contradictions is that each person is a bundle of contradictions. In a contradiction, the two sides are meeting. An opposition is happening – it has come alive with great tension and energy.

Balance brings equilibrium to contradictions. But balance includes passion, movement, rhythm, urgency and harmony. Balance is not an imposed thing, such as repression or fear, nor is it a purely subjective thing. Balance is an implicit equilibrium that emerges in the fair-play of opposing forces. Balance yields itself in the dialogue of passionate forces. Balance is linked to listening and attentiveness. True balance is a grace.

But there are several agents of imbalance today. One is the whole consumerist trend of post-modern culture. Key conversations are not taking place – between the privileged and the poor, between the western culture and Islam, between the forces of the city culture and the rural domain.

Ireland has been in turbulence, corruption has been revealed, and this has dulled and damaged our sense of and belief in ideals. But the positive side of this is that it relieves us of over-dependence on false crutches; it invites us to depend more on our own courage and critique. Our tradition has huge spiritual, imaginative and wisdom riches. There was a sense of proportion, a sense of belonging, a sense of being in a tradition that we are now in danger of losing completely. We need great vision and leadership to engage all the tensions of the present turbulence and find a path that vitally connects with the heart of the Irish tradition and yet engages the modern milieu openly and creatively.

Balance and difference were also central to the ideas of composer and pianist **Mícheál Ó Súilleabháin**, who reported that part of the necessary wisdom of the time we live in is an understanding of the dynamic between the local and the global:

How do we make the movement between what we were, what we are and what we are becoming? Listening to the difference between the local and the global is like listening to the difference between self and other.

> *'Linking the global to the local remains pregnant with meaning and relevance'*

The balance between locus and globus is a key to unlocking those connections, the key to the music within, the key to making the body of the culture start to sing again. Linking the global to the local may be something of a cliché now, but it is one that remains pregnant with meaning and relevance. Someone once amalgamated those words to 'glocal', but that has a hardness.

Ó Súilleabháin was drawn towards the different amalgamation of 'lobal': quite apart from its softness, 'lobal' carries resonances of the lobe of the ear.

We must search out the boundaries of difference. In one sense, what we do is what we are. And how we do it is what we do. Human doing is human being. And human being is manifest in the rituals of artistic expression in a unique way. We must reteach ourselves and teach our children how to express themselves, how to find freedom of voice through freedom of choice. This is the heart of the matter – the show of humanity – the saying, the singing, the moving, the sounding, the tracing, the marking, the making – all putting out the human hearts on display.

Human imagination is as limitless as the mystery of that outer universe, and that imagination finds reflection in the inner world of each human body. These rituals of embodied human communication, in poetry, storytelling, music, dance, in how we choose to build our houses and temples, in how we cultivate the soil – all these speak of an agriculture of the soul, of the inner spark or spirit, of the digging of the humus through the emotional leaves of our lives that we display and shed, and through the ultimate humility that brings us to our knees despite ourselves in the face of life and nature.

Shared artistic ritual allows us to descend into the valleys of artistic communication. We come to love these valleys, these poems, this music, that dance, those places, ourselves, We own them as we own up to them. They are our vales of honey, our sun palaces, our 'bailes' and townlands of the familiar, the soundscape of our lives – a home to go to, a warmth, a comfort, a womb with a view! These are our traditions, our inheritances, our heritage, things passed through and passed on. They identify us, they are our dynamic selves.

But behind these differences and contradictions lie severe disturbances, with awkward questions to be asked, said psychologist and writer **Janet Murray**, claiming that there is evidence in our culture of deep unease:

We have the highest consumption of alcohol per capita of almost any industrial country. For example, we have three times the per capita consumption of the Germans. We have also a clearly identified pattern of binge drinking on a scale unmatched elsewhere. Also, there is evidence of the over-representation of the Irish as an ethnic group in statistics on admissions to mental health facilities worldwide, above that of other migrant groups.

What is most striking is our collective refusal to explore the real psychological roots of this long-standing distressed and distressing behaviour. We display a general lack of psychological curiosity about it. Indeed, to think and speculate in psychological terms at all is regarded in our culture with suspicion. The negative stigma we generate in relation to mental health issues and those afflicted by them is matched only by our refusal to think psychologically about social and personal issues.

There are some awkward questions to be asked. If community values of old were so important and dear to us then why have so many of us colluded in their near abandonment? How have we done this on so many levels? Is it possible that little real or authentic community ever existed, that there was little emotional contact taking place? Might this explain how quickly the appearance of community was abandoned? Or was it that instead of authentic communication and sharing between people we had merely a sense of solidarity in poverty, an interdependence that rarely

'Is it possible that little real or authentic community ever existed?'

went further than functional co-operation? If the elderly were ever valued and revered and included in our communities as we tell ourselves they were, then why have we now shunted them to one side so quickly and treat them as irrelevant to our collective pursuits? The notion of family has always been held up as an ideal, as an answer to all manner of social problems. Yet there was always so much going on in families that did not fit with this idealisation. The family is a complex entity. The surface appearance and what is supposed to happen is very different to what really transpires. The truth about family is held by all of us as private knowledge that finds little space in the public sphere. If we can be nurtured in families we can also be destroyed in families. Our culture does not permit the more complex reading of family and its potential difficulties. Why is this so? Are we afraid of the necessary depression that such public disillusionment around family might bring?

Certainly in the past we afflicted ourselves with impossible ideals and impossible loyalties resulting in the splitting of the psyche between light and dark, good and bad, sober and drunk, outwardly conformist and inwardly rebellious. Is this splitting still going on in a more disguised form? Do we find it difficult to be whole people in the world rather than split people? Are we afraid that we might become too boring to ourselves if we become whole? Are we afraid to be criticised, to have to stand alone without defences, just as we are? Hand-wringing and blaming always seem preferable to any kind of accurate self-reflection, to the hard work of seeing our part in the way things are. It is only when we give up our blaming of others, of circumstances, of fate, and take responsibility for how we are now and what we have created, that we make progress. What we have is what we want. It must be the case. There is nobody to blame. It is not easy to stop blaming. It is not easy to see our part in things as they are. But that is the only way that personal change or any real change takes place.

Economic Growth is Only Part of the Solution

Complementing the concerns for values – both the 'soul for Ireland' of the religious, and the 'the answer lies in our humanity' of the secular – was a strong scepticism about economic growth. Within both perspectives was a strong view that economic growth, while bringing benefits, is not the solution to everything. Economics writer **Richard Douthwaite** highlighted that economic growth provides only part of the answer to today's challenges, claiming that it had not brought improvements in the lives of ordinary citizens:

Growth brought extra business profits and more jobs. But that was paid for through lower wages and greater job insecurity because of the way the globalised economic system worked. Benefits of growth have hefty price tags: firms are constantly trying to lower their costs; growth has become dependent on more investment and consumer spending. Because of this, governments have a vested interest in ensuring that growth continues, irrespective of its benefits.

It is impossible to say where the extra income generated by growth has gone. A major chunk has gone to transnational companies and to the richest 30 per cent of the population. Reflecting this, Ireland has the second-least equal distribution of earnings among the member states of the OECD. In Ireland, the rich have got richer and the poor have got poorer in relation to the rich. There is evidence that in countries where incomes have become more equal, the incidence of disease has fallen and life expectancy has gone up. There is evidence that the best way to make people feel better is not to produce more and more goods for them to consume, but to share incomes, and therefore goods, more equally.

For example, in the US it has been found that states with greater inequality of income have a greater proportion of problems associated with poor health, crime, homicide, disability

> **'Growth became our master rather than our servant'**

and social conditions. Likewise, in Ireland, there is evidence of a worsening of social indicators, showing that the well-being of Irish people has been declining since the 1970s.

Growth in employment in the 1990s was powered by an unprecedented spending spree, fuelled by people getting themselves or their companies heavily into debt. Because of the property boom, people on the average industrial wage found themselves priced completely out of the market. The need for growth got in the way of the needs of ordinary people. Growth became our master rather than our servant. The method Ireland was using to generate growth could not be continued. The distribution of income here is already the second worst in the developed world and cannot be skewed much further without society tearing itself apart. Also, we have had a total failure to keep our greenhouse emissions in check.

The reason we are emotionally attached to growth and why we find it so hard to say it should stop is that everybody feels that if they had a little bit more of something they would be better off. What we fail to realise is that what is possible for one person is probably not possible for all, and if everybody gets a little bit more it may alter or destroy not only the expected benefits but also those that people enjoyed before the change. Similarly, if the process of growth alters the distribution of income in a country – and particularly if it makes it less equitable as it has done in Ireland – we cannot conclude that, just because overall consumption is higher, overall well-being has gone up too.

The first thing we need to do to achieve a better balance between our economic and social objectives, and between our economic system and the planet's environment, is to accept that the rate of increase in national income is a very poor guide to anything at all except the potential for making a profit. Once we have accepted that the annual growth figure is largely of interest to the business community and a very poor guide to anything for anyone else, we ought to calculate an annual Index of Sustainable Economic Welfare for Ireland to see whether the quest for growth is making this country less sustainable. The third step is to work out just what it is about our economic system that causes it to crash into a depression if a minimum rate of growth is not achieved. The fourth step is to realise that the resources we are using to generate growth each year could be used in other ways. We could use the resources we're devoting to growth to cure poverty more directly. We need to move to a stable, sustainable – and that means zero-growth – world and move away from the current system of economic growth of any sort where the market generated was seen as the greatest good.

This limited role of the market and the economy was also argued by **Robert Lane**, professor of political science at Yale University, who told of evidence that, as the material standard of living increases, the alternative goods that become more appealing are not things you can buy in the market, rather they are things like friendship and family felicity:

As money and what you can do with money become relatively more abundant compared with these non-market goods, the relative value of money declines and the relative value of people and their companionship increases. Thus, in any trade-off between the two goods, money and companionship, where money is relatively plentiful and companionship relatively scarce, companionship will add more to subjective well-being than money. Quality of life studies in America show that satisfying family life plus relations with friends contribute more to subjective well-being than do satisfaction with standard of living. In these cases, companionship makes a larger contribution to satisfaction than income.

'Companionship will add more to subjective well-being than money'

There is evidence of the development of a new stage markedly different from previous stages. This includes diminished priority for economic efficiency and growth, rejection of both religious authority and absolute moral values, tolerance for ethnic minorities and for deviance from sexual and other norms, with an emphasis on better human relations and warm communal ties. There is a growing emphasis on individual autonomy and reliance on the informative value of a person's own experience as contrasted to orthodoxies of all kinds. The evidence is that the richer the country and the younger the people involved, the more is the emphasis on values like these.

But there is a puzzle. Advanced societies are now at a threshold of a New Humanism where persons and companionship can take the place of things and their acquisition. Markets have made us rich enough so that we can afford to follow a social rather than a materialist programme. At long last, we can put human qualities and our preferences for other human beings at the centre of things. But the market economics that brought us here inhibits the exercise of these preferences, partly by requiring us, as a condition of our wealth, to continue to place a high premium on money and to make this sacrifice gladly.

The dangers of these market economics were also emphasised by director of the Centre for Transition Studies and Textual Studies at Dublin City University, **Michael Cronin**, who spoke of how we have moved from a society that was producer-centred to one that is consumer-centred:

People have increasingly been defined less and less by what they do and more and more by what they consume. What are the consequences of that shift from production to consumption? If you take consumption, once you buy goods or a service, that is it. The transaction is over from your point of view as a consumer. However, if you look at it from the point of view of production, the experience is radically different, because the difference between consumption and production is that production is a relationship that endures. There are three things that characterise production. The first is confidence. The second is trust and the third is obligation. Confidence, because if you produce something, whether it is goods or services, you have to have confidence that what you are making or what you are offering is something that is going to last, that is going to endure. Trust, because when you produce something, you are indebted to or reliant on other people in order for the good to be produced or the service to be provided. Third, the notion of obligation is the obligation that you bring to the task in hand whether it is production of the goods or offering the service, the idea that you will do something.

So these three notions of confidence, trust and obligation are things that are intrinsic to the production process. So if we have a society that shifts from being production-centred to being consumption-centred, we have to be concerned as to what happens to those notions of confidence, trust and obligation.

There are a number of consequences that can be identified. The notion of short-termism, a certain distrust of others, a lack of trust, the lack of confidence in the future. The networks of dependency in society are important because in an age of individualism, very often what is stressed is the notion of independence, which is seen as a way of rejecting older forms of dependence, especially interdependence.

'What happens to confidence, trust and obligation?'

Other issues include the 'tyranny of the moment'. We have to spend more and more time processing or dealing with information – emails, meetings, communications; all these information-processing activities are taking up more and more of our time. It becomes increasingly difficult to think about the future, and indeed it becomes increasingly difficult to make sense of the present.

However, the positive contribution of economic growth in previous years was emphasised by economic consultant and journalist **Paul Tansey**, who demonstrated the benefits of such growth and how this has given a valuable legacy for the years ahead. Tansey reported that, as a sovereign state, Ireland has suffered long spells of economic failure, most notably in the first forty years of its existence:

> 'Ireland's economic success in the 1990s was wedded to its embracing a culture of openness'

The social impacts of that failure – mass emigration, population decline, poverty – provide little reason for nostalgia. Moreover it is important that we recall the values that gave rise to failure: a closed, inward-looking, rigid authoritarianism that suppressed not only the free play of ideas but the emergence of a properly functioning market economy. Ireland's economic success in the 1990s had been wedded to its embracing a culture of openness – openness to trade, openness to foreign investment, openness to immigration and openness to new and competing ideas.

However, the incidence of poverty was then reported by Tansey to have been still significant:

There is a considerable proportion who are economically vulnerable with low relative incomes, experience difficulty in making ends meet and are at risk of deprivation and income poverty. A key problem is the continued existence of concentrated geographic areas of multiple deprivation. These are areas where poverty is entrenched and disadvantage is multi-dimensional.

Outside the area of poverty, Ireland's broad social performance was reported to have been impressive:

In terms of quality of life during the past decade, Ireland ranked fourth in the Human Development Index after Norway, Iceland and Australia. The HDI is compiled by the United Nations Development Programme (UNDP). The variables it used in assessing quality of life are: income per head; life expectancy; years of schooling; and adult literacy.

Amongst countries that are not tax havens, Ireland has enjoyed the third highest purchasing power per head of population in the world after the United States and Norway. These data are adjusted for differences in national price levels to give a more accurate assessment of command over goods and services.

Ireland ranks fourth in terms of equal development opportunities for men and women. The Gender-Related Development Index, also compiled by the UNDP, finds that disparities in human development opportunities for men and women in Ireland are smaller than in all countries bar Norway, Iceland and Australia. In the sphere of child well-being, Ireland ranks ninth among the twenty-one most advanced industrial countries. Ireland rates particularly well in the areas of the educational well-being of children and the supportive environment of family and friends; but much less well in terms of the material well-being of children and children's health. Ireland is thirteenth in the league of the largest bilateral and multilateral foreign aid donors (aid as percentage of GDP), ahead of Germany and Japan. Ireland has the third lowest divorce rate in Europe, after Bosnia and Georgia, and the thirteenth lowest divorce rate in the world.

In the context of the current recession, economist and lecturer **Jim Power** said that the changed economic reality had brought a lot of pressures, but that these would hopefully bring a much greater sense of reality and sanity to the situation:

What can we do to engage, address or ease these pressures? Coming at this from a very economic perspective, it is clear that people need to refocus on personal financial planning and budgeting: getting debt levels down is absolutely essential.

People need to change their spending behaviour. We will need to prioritise our requirements, which is something many of us did not have to do in the Celtic Tiger era. We need to start ignoring the Joneses. We certainly need to adjust our expectations to new economic and financial realities. Above all else, we need to keep an incredibly strong focus on education as a society. Investment in education has been seriously lagging in recent years. If Ireland is to re-emerge from the current economic situation intact, it is the quality of people that will determine our success or failure. The focus on the quality of education is absolutely essential. Society is obviously significantly more important than an economy, but a well-managed, sane economy is essential for a society. A society needs an economy, an economy needs a society; the two are not mutually exclusive.

> *'We need to adjust our expectations to new economic and financial realities'*

We need to distinguish between economic activity and economic welfare. Welfare is a measure of well-being and happiness; economic activity is a financial measure that tells us nothing about the quality of life. We need to focus more on quality of life than on quantity of economic growth. We have made a lot of mistakes and we have created significant pressures on family life. But we may hopefully be moving back into a sphere where there is going to be a much greater focus on community, society and quality of life, rather than the quantity of economic growth.

Conclusion
Here, thus, is a unity of the Christian and the humanist around the two themes of inner identity and collective potential. These values are integrated into public policy via social capital, the resourcing of

individuals, and power and leadership – themes that will form the basis of the subsequent chapters.

TWO

Social Capital

Social capital is about our stock of shared values, social networks and connections. But this valuable resource is being threatened by several forces such as individualistic lifestyles and more complicated patterns of social interaction. In the face of this, we need to revalue the ethic of care and place fresh emphasis on the public policies that support social capital.

Social Capital in the United States: Loss of Connections

Political scientist **Robert Putnam** explained social capital in simple terms and looked to its manifestation in America:

This is what economists call the externalities of social networks. In an organisation or community where there is a dense network of social connections – where people are connected to one another – what tends to evolve is a norm of reciprocity, generalised reciprocity. This means that I will do something for you now without expecting something immediately back from you, because down the road you will do something for me, and you will do something for him, because we will all see each other at church on Sunday. Social capital is, in short, networks and reciprocity and what goes along with that – trust and trustworthiness.

> *'Social capital is networks, reciprocity, trust and trustworthiness'*

If we look at membership of social organisations we find that for most of the twentieth century, Americans, year by year, were becoming more 'joiners'. Almost every organisation in America

– for example, parents associations, youth clubs, business groups – increased its membership substantially especially between the end of the Second World War and the mid-1960s. But then suddenly all of these organisations started experiencing a fall in membership until by the end of the twentieth century the United States had dropped to comparatively very low levels of organisational activity.

The same story emerges when we look at studies of changing lifestyle of Americans. These show that every single community activity measured in the surveys is down over the course of the last thirty years – going to meetings, being part of a local organisation. Over the course of the last three decades, about half of all the civic infrastructure of American communities simply evaporated. All sorts of voluntary organisations simply disappeared. The surveys show that virtually every form of social connection measured is down substantially – club meetings, dinner parties, card playing, picnics, having friends to your house. There has also been a steady decline in attendance at church.

There are many other ways in which this general phenomenon has made itself manifest. One is that America has become a less generous society. As we stopped going to club meetings and church, we have become less generous. Another result is that we trust one another less. In the 1960s, more than half of Americans said that most people could be trusted. Now it is down to one-third. This trend of growing distrust is concentrated among America's young people. In their view, they are growing up in a less trustworthy society.

Suburbanisation is a factor, with every ten minutes of additional commuting time cutting all forms of social connection by an equivalent proportion. Movement of women into the paid labour force is also a factor, but not as much as most people think. Television also turns out to be an important contributor to the decline in social connectivity – commercial entertainment television is lethal for social connection.

Decline in connectivity is experienced by different income groups and ethnic groups. However, one group is exceptional – older people. The group of Americans who came of age before or during World War II were much more socially connected. That generation was terrific about civic engagement, but they did not pass it on to their children or their grandchildren.

There are costs deriving from this loss of social connectedness. In many measurable ways societies do not work as well when we are not connected with one another – crime, success at school, physical health, depression, all of these are influenced positively by social connectedness.

'We need to invent new ways of connecting'

What do we do about this? We, in America, need to invent new ways of connecting that fit into the way that we have come to live and this will involve changes at the grassroots. It will also involve initiatives by government. There needs to be policy changes in America, for example changes that will affect the balance between work and life; how do we fit work and life obligations when both parents are working outside the home? This is partly a problem for employers and partly a problem for government. Also there are things that people can do. There are things that need to be done at the grassroots in reweaving the fabric of our society. We need to figure out new ways to create a wider 'sense of us', new ways of connecting with other people, formally and informally, and reweaving the fabrics of our societies, not in traditional ways, but in new ways that will last us for decades.

Social Capital in Ireland: Rich but Weakening?

The transformation of Ireland has been intense, according to psychologist, writer and broadcaster **Maureen Gaffney**, who argued that in the future the concept of social capital may be a useful point to organise our thinking about the 'problems' of Irish society:

Decline in social capital matters. High social capital creates a more trusting society, helps with economic prosperity, promotes safe neighbourhoods and encourages physical and psychological health. The decline in social capital has contributed to the relentless privatisation of lifestyle – the retreat into so-called 'lifestyle enclaves' – ever smaller and homogeneous social worlds – at the expense of participation in the larger public community.

Irish society is regarded as rich in social capital. But there are some symptoms of the depletion of social capital. While Irish society is still very intimate and connected, the old ways of connecting have been weakened and reliable new ways have yet to be forged. Our society will have to realise that the old order is indeed gone and that what is required is a project for value regeneration that will replenish the social capital. But that regeneration must be in tune with the modern age.

We need to revalue the ethic of care in structuring the relationship between the individual and the larger community. We place such value on autonomy, rights, rules and procedures that status in our society is largely coming to be measured by the degree of autonomy an individual can achieve from obligations and intrusions. If we were more focused on the ethic of care, on the other hand, we would place more societal value on the forming and maintenance of close intimate relationships with others, on connection for its own sake. From this perspective, success and status would also be measured by the degree of closeness achieved, by the fulfilling of responsibilities to others.

> **'We need to revalue the ethic of care'**

We must find a way to articulate the ethic of care in a way that touches peoples' lives in a real way, so that people can imagine and experience what acting in a caring way means. The concept of caring should tap into the cardinal civic virtues that are essential for the common good – the generous impulse, the readiness to be compassionate, the readiness to modulate self-interest, the sense of fair play, the sense of duty. What is needed is an organisational mechanism, a connective tissue that will unite these civic virtues into an effective, coherent force for the pursuit of justice and social solidarity.

Tom Healy of the Department of Education and Science spoke of the impact social capital has on a nation's well-being:

The evidence for declining social capital is much less clear in Europe and other parts of the industrialised world. The suggestions point towards stability in many of the standard measures of social capital, although one apparent exception is the level of interpersonal trust and especially trust towards institutions. We are certainly much more aware of the extent and prevalence of corruption and other anti-social behaviour.

The term 'human capital' was coined by economists in the early 1960s to recognise the key importance of knowledge and skills in contributing to economic well-being. Human capital is the property of individuals, while social capital is the property of groups, communities and organisations. This is defined as networks together with shared norms, values and understanding that facilitate co-operation within or among groups. The use of the concept of social capital is important as it draws attention to the benefits and costs of relating to others in a way that can help individuals, groups, communities and governments to invest more wisely.

As citizens, we care about the cohesiveness of society and each other's well-being. A broad view of well-being goes beyond market measures. There is evidence that, beyond a certain threshold, income matters less for life satisfaction than other factors. It appears that the quality of interpersonal relationships and social ties, together with important life events such as unemployment, education, divorce and

'Quality of interpersonal relationships and social ties become critical'

health, become critical. Thus, beyond a certain level of income, there is increased satisfaction from better health, education and especially better quality relations with others. Insights from psycho-social research have refocused attention on the role of social ties and norms as important mediating factors in influencing the impact of income, education and employment on physical health and mental well-being. There is also likely to be significant impacts of social capital on economic well-being. Evidence suggests a link between levels of trust and growth as well as levels of trust and investment in physical capital.

A renewed focus on social capital raises general policy design issues. Investing in social and human capital makes good sense for families, communities, business and government – if we can identify what and how to invest time and money. It is likely that social capital in Ireland, as elsewhere, is changing while newer forms of association, involvement and civic engagement are emerging. The challenge is to reconcile what is positive in many of the new forms of association and participation in labour markets and society with a consideration for the wider needs of human well-being and justice. Perhaps the greatest challenge to policy makers is how to bring about 'bridging social capital'. This is the type of social capital in which the focus is on establishing links and reciprocal engagement across different groups, helping transition towards diversity, and pluralism in attitudes and expectations.

Striking an optimistic note, **Tony Fahey** of the Economic and Social Research Institute reported that the survey evidence at the time did not support the theory of general negativism about trends in quality of life in Ireland:

In Ireland, there was no indication of a decline in social capital of the kind that had been identified in the United States. There had been a general improvement in most dimensions of social life as well. This was even taking into account the rising rate of crime, though with regard to rising crime rates, the expectation is that if you were to quantify the history of interpersonal violence in Ireland it would show a less dramatic upward movement than most people would often assume. The level of violence that was practiced with official sanction in the schools in the 1950s requires comparison. It was almost as if violence was applauded – spare the rod and spoil the child.

Irish people continued to be highly sociable and gregarious. Participation in voluntary organisations had been rising, according to the figures. People are quite surprised to hear this because the usual cry is that it is hard to get people to commit themselves to voluntary activity, but the number of voluntary organisations in Ireland over the years had simply exploded. Thus, one of the reasons why people found it hard to man the voluntary organisations is that they were in competition with more voluntary organisations than ever before.

Volunteers: Ambitious and Determined

Volunteering contributes hugely to social capital, and many volunteer groups are ambitious, determined and armed with an agenda they intend to see through, according to then President **Mary McAleese**:

[Volunteers] are plugged into state services, the local community, the churches, the professions, the media, and they are painstakingly creating, developing and sustaining the partnership-driven web of mutual care and support that it takes to get through a tough life with dignity. They leverage extraordinary amounts of money from their own pockets and the pockets of the wider community and government, and they put that money, along with their freely given time, skill and commitment, to knitting all of us together as a community and not just a bunch of indifferent strangers. They teach our kids sport, they donate their blood to our sick, house the homeless, comfort the bereaved, counsel the troubled, feed the hungry, welcome the stranger, care for the environment, get involved in politics. This very day they will do a million good things that will bring joy and comfort, hope and opportunity, courtesy and kindness into the lives of others and they will listen with sinking hearts as their massive contribution, their sacrifice and their considerable faith in humanity is overlooked yet again in discussion about the future direction of our country. They are our hope

'It is in giving that we receive' and our reassurance. They also know something that those who have never volunteered do not yet know – that it really is in giving that we receive, that amidst the many frustrations there is fun, friendship and fulfilment that no shop can sell, no gadget can generate.

Freda Donoghue confirmed this perspective, reporting that voluntary organisations do more than provide services, that they are about citizenship, community belonging and civic expression:

They are one way in which social cohesion is generated and are important building blocks in societal sustainability. Yet volunteering may only be occurring among certain social groups. This raises issues that need to be addressed.

The data shows the power of the voluntary and community sector. Just over 3 per cent of the non-agricultural labour force is in paid employment in the voluntary and community sector but this proportion doubles to almost 6 per cent when voluntary labour is included. The powerhouse of the sector is in all of its employees, the task that these workers perform for the organisations, the responsibilities and the roles that they hold. It is about their value, not only their economic value but their wider value. It is estimated that one-third of all adults are engaged in volunteering in Ireland. However, two-thirds of the population do not engage in volunteering. Non-volunteers are more likely to be male, older or under thirty, with lower educational attainment and in the lower socio-economic group. Thus, the profile of volunteering suggests that those who are aged in their middle years, have a higher educational qualification and higher socio-economic status are most likely to become volunteers. The challenge is thus that there are certain social groups who are not participating as much as others and this may have important implications for social cohesion and social capital.

There is a challenge for voluntary organisations to address these findings, namely that they must adopt creative ways for ensuring volunteering enters the public consciousness. Voluntary organisations need to be more proactive about asking for volunteers.

Volunteering has been defined as the commitment of time and energy for the benefit of society, local communities, and individuals outside the immediate family. Voluntary activities are undertaken of a person's own free will, without payment. Definitions of volunteering are thus based on the individual. Volunteering, therefore, involves the self-engaged in what is generally perceived to a be selfless act that is altruistic, but that is inherently about the self as the definition implies. The motivation to volunteer demonstrates a combination of different factors – idealism, altruism, pragmatism, sense of enjoyment, being part of a network or community. Networks beget networks, participation leads to further participation, involvement aids social cohesion and the sustainability of society.

'Networks beget networks'

Voluntary activity is about society building and society sustaining. It involves the concept of commonality and community. Civic expression means the expression of the civic self, that is the self who is public, associated with the community, or at local level. The importance of the expression of the self in society is about the individual – which volunteering is at some level – entering into relationships. The result is finding expression with others who think or act similarly. This leads to the generation of social groups or social cohesion.

As one aspect of volunteering, the role of 'social entrepreneurship' was highlighted by solicitor **Mary Redmond**, showing that, in the information society, jobs are changing rapidly with a decline in continuous full-time employment and a corresponding surge in atypical work and self-employment:

Work as we know it is being systematically eliminated. Because the importance of formal work in our lives is diminishing, alternative visions must be found. We have heard of the importance of catering for spiritual as well as economic needs, and we must work towards partnerships of different kinds. It is social entrepreneurs who will provide the alternative vision that is needed to complement the information society. Voluntarism brings forth an energy or intensity in the community that is emotional and intellectual.

To those in the voluntary sector, value in life is not solely the attaining of some aim through creating something of material value. For the social entrepreneur the answer consists not in talk and research and position papers but in right action and in right conduct. Innovativeness and vision are essential. Above all, the activity is not for profit. It is the activity of the gift economy: the gift of a person, him or herself, their time, their talents, their energies. When we give of ourselves we truly give.

There is something that is missing in the voluntary sector. It is the gelling of its energy into a powerful countervailing view of the 'voluntary sector', capable of many things, including influencing and even setting the agenda of this nation. The social entrepreneur is not yet the new authority because at present voluntarism is dotted all round the margins of public and private life. In places, volunteerism is strong, in others it is weak. It is organised, it is disorganised. It is big, it is small. It needs to be brought to the centre.

There is a need for alliances between the voluntary and corporate sectors by bringing about a paradigm shift in corporate perceptions of voluntary organisations. Above all, we must overcome the fragmentation of the voluntary sector. Partnership when it comes must be at arm's length, between parties sharing burdens and benefits together. An unequal or fragmented partnership cannot be really effective, and the voluntary sector's lack of cohesion is a serious constraint.

'We must overcome the fragmentation of the voluntary sector'

The structure of volunteerism is not hierarchical. Equality between groups, big and small, is vital. Other values too are important, such as autonomy, diversity and the friendship of networking. Coming together will mean personal transformation, together with community and environmental change. Voluntary groups themselves will benefit from greater cohesiveness. The information society offers wondrous possibilities for creative change. The proper place for and role of the voluntary sector should be one of them.

Social Capital and the Family: Central to the Agenda

Apart from volunteering, the family was frequently cited as a central element in the social capital agenda. For example, **Cardinal Seán Brady** claimed that there are few institutions more important to the future of our society than the family, but also few that have been subject to such rapid and fundamental change:

The prospect of a married couple establishing a happy, loving and stable family home in Ireland today has never been greater. The challenge is to help women and men secure the life-long fulfilment it can offer, especially those who are reluctant to make a life-long commitment. The family is the natural community in which human social nature is experienced. It makes a unique and irreplaceable contribution to the good of society. The family unit is borne from the stable and committed communion of persons that marriage provides. 'Communion' has to do with the personal relationship between the 'I' and the 'thou'. 'Community', on the other hand, transcends the 'I' and the 'thou' and moves towards a society – a 'we'. The family, therefore, as a community of persons, is the first human 'society'. It is at the very heart of the common good.

Marriage and the family, therefore, are of public interest. They are fundamental to the public good and entitled to special consideration and care from the state. Life-long marriage remains the preferred choice of the vast majority of men and women in Ireland. 'Family capital' is at the core of 'social capital', upon which we build the future of our country. Marriage deserves to be supported by society. It is so fundamental to the common good that the state acts in the interests of society when it supports marriage through benefits in taxation, social welfare and social policy. We also need to provide greater support for married couples as they live out their life-long commitment to each other and their children.

The role of altruism in the family had significant implications for the development of social capital, according to psychologist and writer **Marie Murray**, who spoke of how forms of family vary and how we need ways to traverse and support all children in every family form, so that children are equipped with the resilience of belief in themselves, respect for others, participation in the community and the feelings of self-worth that derive from community involvement:

One of the distinguishing characteristics of children in challenging family forms is that they often feel they do not belong anywhere. If there is one thing a child needs when their needs are not being met, it is to belong to someone or something and to have a role in life. This is where giving children the joy of altruism, that extraordinary consciousness of the needs of others, can give them a sense of self-esteem, worth and purpose in life. It can provide them with a belief that who they are and what they do has positive meaning for other people and that they have value and a contribution to make to the world.

Introducing children to altruism may be an important therapeutic and significant psychological intervention when life is difficult for them. Although altruism may be viewed as a philosophical disposition, as an ideological principle, or as an abstract or unpractical approach to the needs of children, when it is modelled, nurtured into a personal value system, assisted into practical activity and given appropriate expression in a community, the consequence is a binding with others and growth in the child of a sense of personal value and relevance. A child who is without self-esteem may receive it from giving it to others. That is the paradox; that is its power; that is its simple rationale. Pro-social behaviour promotes self-esteem. Therefore, if we ask what will assist children in coping with the diversity of family life today, inviting them to be altruistic may be one way of assisting them. It is one perspective, one parenting precept, one potential means of social cohesion: an emotional and behavioural approach that deserves careful consideration at this time. In the 'Great Revolution' of family life, simple gentle attention to altruism may be the key.

'Giving children the joy of altruism'

Altruism is usually defined as behaviour motivated by concern for others. Altruism does not depend on systems of reward or punishment but contains within itself its own reward. It is gentle. It is spiritual. It is transcendent. It lifts children out of egocentricity. It takes adolescents away from egoism and puts adults back in touch with the finer aspects of themselves.

Social Capital in the Wider Community: The Ebb and Flow of Relationships

Both privatisation and the growth of the state have important consequences for local communities, according to economist **Finola Kennedy**, who highlighted that we are part of the global economy:

To grow means simply to increase in size. With growth we have lost our small national schools, our local garda stations, our small post offices and neighbourhood letterboxes. Postal collections and deliveries are reduced. Sole practice GPs are vanishing. House calls by GPs are virtually extinct. The days of small hospitals are numbered. Children are bussed to bigger and more distant schools. All of this growth in the size of service delivery units is done in the name of efficiency. Certainly there is justification for rationalisation but hardly for all the 'rationalisation' of services, especially when reduction of services is accompanied by an increase in bureaucracy. Bureaucracy itself, often riding on the back of some worthy and expensive consultancy report, can then become itself the problem. And a new phenomenon has emerged with the growth of bureaucracy – the replacement of human beings at the end of phone lines with prerecorded menus interspersed with tunes.

'Reduction in services is accompanied by an increase in bureaucracy'

The ebb and flow of personal relationships is not independent from the socio-economic currents. In some important respects those currents have been flowing in opposite directions. Today, when the role of state enterprise has been removed or reduced mainly due to privatisation, the role of the state in providing 'home' services has never been more extensive. A curious shift is taking place: as the economy moves more in the direction of private enterprise and the market, more Boston than Berlin, many traditional functions of the home are shifting towards the state. The move out of the home to service the economy is having the effect of increasing demands on the state for services previously provided on a voluntary basis at home.

At the same time, it would be false to make distinctions that are too rigid. Just as 'private enterprise' is supported by a plethora of grants and tax breaks, so too private individuals are helped in their caring functions by supports that include child benefit and carer's allowance. The state also assists the private provision of, for example, hospitals and crèches, via major tax breaks. The provision of crèches and homes for the elderly is big business today.

Accompanying the shift towards the provision by the state of services formerly provided by people in their own homes, or frequently by religious orders and voluntary groups, there has been a shift in policy towards the prioritisation of market work over work in homes. For example, the individualisation of the tax system has provided incentives for labour force, as distinct from household work. Childcare is an issue for bosses as well as babies and their parents.

Who will care for the children and the elderly? These are key questions and how they are addressed reflects the relative priority that we attach to paid work and to family life in its widest sense. What is the relative respect that society really accords to the largely voluntary work within the household, as distinct from paid work in the workplace? In a fundamental way, in the sense of creating a social environment, embedded in a safe and secure physical environment, in which it is possible for lives to be lived and for people to die within a network of relationships that are intimate enough to be human, we need to create a 'social village', with some of the features of the old village. This should be a society in which both government and governed share a common purpose and participation in that enterprise is facilitated at local level. At the core of the social network is the family unit, however broadly

'This should be a society in which both government and governed share a common purpose'

or narrowly defined. From that intimate nucleus grows true citizenship. If opportunity and responsibility are reflected in how we design our provision and taxation system, then community will develop.

Modern technology opens a world of opportunity. The internet can be used to make and retain contacts. Local radio is of great value in forming and strengthening communities and has potential for further development. Voluntary activity as a facet of active citizenship is available to all who are able and who wish to participate. If everyone who is able to do so were to join one of the multitude of voluntary organisations that exist in the country and give a minimum of two hours per week in some work of service, the country and its citizens would be transformed.

The global value of community as a source of social capital was addressed by **Ray Kinsella** and **Maurice Kinsella** of University College Dublin, who reported that the global economic crisis had its roots in an ethical catharsis:

The corporate ethos within which the crisis was incubated subverted the very idea of community. The idea of community might be broadly defined as a group of individuals animated by shared and objective values and which is shaped by an innate understanding and acceptance of the common good. Community makes demands on us – it takes us beyond the 'I' to the 'we'. It includes, but is not limited to, mutuality of interest.

The global crisis was essentially about right and wrong. It was about a clash between an ethical system rooted in objective values based on the transcendent value of the human person, and philosophies based on relativism and a depersonalisation of the whole productive process. It was reflected in a subversion of markets in which products that had no reality to the productive process dwarfed the real economy and played havoc with businesses and with the lives of individuals and families.

Community can be defined as service to our neighbour. It is about looking out for each other, recognising that we are mutually dependent. It exists at every level of the activities in which we engage: from our own individual families, through friendships and into economic activities. Community exists within universities and hospitals and, of course, religious communities. It is what holds us together as persons of equal dignity.

The economic crisis fractured and subverted the idea of community, not least in Ireland. This is because no community that defines itself in terms of individuals of equal dignity and worth can exist in an environment characterised by lies, greed, power and self-serving interests that are nascent in all of us but which took tangible form in the causes of the economic crisis.

It follows that part of the recovery from the traumatic effects across countries, as well as here in Ireland, is the rediscovery of 'community' as the indispensible basis of a sustainable and values-based economy and, by extension, society. We need to re-discover community and all that it implies in terms of a leadership based on service, rather than on power, and on respect for the other person, particularly the marginalised. It would not be an overstatement to say that the failure to understand the importance of community is the greatest single threat to the stability of individual countries and to the stability of the global world of which we are all part. Without community, we default back to our own interests and we make the needs and rights of others subservient to our own. This brings its own inevitable consequences.

We need a new politics. We need a leadership of service to the person. The core problem is that the political establishment is not about community or the common good, but about power and patronage. We need local democratic structures and to emphatically reject the culture of dependency on the state, which is the very antithesis of community.

'We need a leadership of service'

This significance of social capital in the wider society was also emphasised by **John Lonergan**, then governor of Mountjoy Prison, who said that there is a singular absence of serious reflection on the whole purpose and meaning of life in holistic terms:

One of the most negative aspects of our current laissez-faire philosophy is that it encourages abdication of responsibility for the direction and well-being of society. It encourages the *mé-féiners*, those who close their eyes and ears to what is happening around them, and who can, thanks to that philosophy, passively ignore the wrongs and injustices rampant throughout society. We selfishly demand more and more 'rights' whilst continually ignoring our responsibilities.

The importance of the family unit in Irish society contributed enormously to the quality of life of past generations. However, the nature of the family is undergoing a huge upheaval. The traditional two-parent, child-oriented family is no longer the norm. The number of dysfunctional families is on the increase. We must never assume that just because we are among people it follows automatically that there is a sense of belonging. The human need to relate to other human beings is a most natural one. It seems that the only listening facilities available in modern Ireland are those provided by the professional listeners, one of the fastest expanding industries of this decade.

The old concept of the local community is also being threatened. We all need to develop a sense of identity and belonging, and the local community once provided a platform for this. Are we losing our sense of community? Are we imprisoning ourselves in our own homes and consciously shutting out our neighbours? Indeed, does such a species exist anymore? We have huge numbers of young and old people who simply cannot cope on their own. Handouts are not the answer. The long-term solution depends on a more compassionate and caring society.

Public campaigns have understandably sought improved childcare facilities, but what about the thousands of young mothers who assume the responsibility of caring for their children without any training or support? We provide little support for young parents, particularly those in our most socially disadvantaged areas. The huge expansion of the nursing home industry is another symptom of our soulless society. Nursing homes are often the only option available but this is not always the case and regrettably in too many instances it is the only option considered. Nursing homes are often lonely places for elderly people. One demand to hit the public arena was the issue of paying our home carers. Is caring for our own families now to become a business?

Our education system is directly totally in favour of the upper classes insofar as it is very much achievement-oriented. Consequently, third-level points are developing into a type of snobbery league. Our educational system has not only failed miserably to bridge the gap between the 'haves' and the 'have nots' but is sustaining it.

Lonergan said he had a unique opportunity of observing 'justice' in action. He met many people who ended up in prison not because they were criminal or dangerous but because there was no other place to care for them, many totally helpless and inadequate:

The direct relationship between drugs and crime is well documented. Many crime problems are interwoven with the drug problems. Only a hypocritical, heartless and soulless society could sleep easily in the midst of such human suffering and despair. The whole issue of professional and white collar crime has been very much in the public domain, but Ireland continues to treat this type of crime quite differently to petty crime. Why?

Creating an acceptable image is high on the priority list of most public representatives, industrialists, financial organisations and the consumer industry. How can Ireland have any degree of public transparency while the professional image-maker has such a prominent role in modern society? The media has been given the huge responsibility of being society's main watchdog and influencer. But the media must not use this power as a weapon to destroy people who criticise it.

'Ireland is a very fragmented society'

Currently Ireland is a very fragmented society – a society divided by self-interest groups who shout at each other but refuse to listen. We need to bring about genuine human inclusiveness and togetherness. We need reconciliation.

The role of social capital in support for people with special needs was emphasised by **Mary Kealy**, chief executive of the Brothers of Charity, who stated that people who experience disabilities and their families are not a special interest group:

They are an ordinary, everyday interest group. Most parents want the chance to raise their young children at home. They want their children to play and learn alongside typically developing children in their local neighbourhoods and schools. When children with disabilities become adults, they want to follow their wishes and dreams, choose a career, go to college and have the chance to make a contribution to the wider community. They want real jobs for real pay in the real world. They want the chance to live in safe, affordable housing, no different to the housing that everyone else enjoys, and they want to be able to choose who to live with, or perhaps just to have a place of their own.

Look at how we deliver support to people, in general, in the human services field, for example, mental health, child welfare, housing, the elderly, juvenile justice and, indeed, adult justice systems. Our approach is to place people with 'one of their own kind', often building a 'special world'. Put more crudely, we design and build housing ghettos, disability ghettos, special units, prisons, thereby creating institutions of all shapes and sizes, so that once you get into them, it is very hard to get out. Remember, institutionalisation is not just about buildings, it becomes a state of mind. Money needs to be invested wisely, in ways that help people assume personal responsibility and participate fully in community life. We do not want our resources to be used for services and supports that foster dependence and isolation. In services for people with an intellectual disability, institutions and large residential settings are places that people went to in the past for security, continuity and safety. In our experience they are places where people are living dangerously, are assaulted frequently by others and where people are living broken lives. The same goes to a lesser extent for mini-institutions, for example, group homes, sheltered workshops and day activity centres.

'Move services and supports out into the community'
The solution is to move services and supports out into the community. We also need to ensure that the managers and service resources that are moving out are helping to build capacity in the community. In essence, we want people in care to have the preciousness of belonging, the awakening of what we can contribute and receive, discovering or re-discovering each other, being valued, being connected and living in companionship.

Social capital in the inter-generational context was cited by **Mary Surlis**, Adult and Community Education Project Officer in NUI Galway, who considered how rapid social and economic developments have contributed to new and more complicated patterns of social interactions:

A more individualistic and impersonal lifestyle is beginning to emerge as we increasingly move away from face-to-face relationships with our neighbours and other people in our communities. There seems to be a retreat from the common good, greater alienation among large sections of our society, an increase in personal isolation and a decrease in social capital.

Social capital refers to the level and extent of social interactions within society. In essence, social capital means the scale of our relationships with other people and our involvement within networks. These networks may be work-based, recreational, religious or family-based. In the context of social capital, pilot initiatives have included inter-generational collaborative projects to provide a learning experience on the extended family, specifically the influence of the grandparent on the extended family. The aim is to promote the sharing of culture, heritage, tradition and experiences between two diverse generations through a structured programme of work. In doing this the perceived barriers of age and social background are addressed. The curriculum process is consultative and participative in nature, and aims to promote reciprocal learning and experience.

In terms of learning outcomes, the inter-generational focus of projects such as these seek to create a climate in which the participants will develop interpersonal skills, self-realisation, character-building skills, cross-generational awareness and respect, which are developed in practical terms through application and self-expression in specific structured modules.

As an example of social capital in the community, then chairman of the Revenue Commissioners, **Frank Daly** claimed that tax is not merely a business cost, not merely a drag on business and the individual:

It is the contribution that we all make to the common good – it is how public services, infrastructure, security, economic policy and even government itself is funded. In simple terms, there are three broad consequences if an individual or business does not pay: the contribution of others is increased, services for others are not delivered or investment in our future is curtailed. Tax is not something forced upon the people by somebody over which they have no control. In our democratic society we elect government and in doing so we give them a mandate that includes setting taxation policy. Readers will be familiar with the principle, first enshrined in the Magna Carta and later employed as a rallying cry in the American Revolution, of 'no taxation without representation'. It is also worth considering the corollary – that democratic representation is dependent on taxation.

Reflecting this, there is a close linkage between social capital and effective government and a US study concluded that 'social capital' is the only factor that successfully predicts tax compliance. A related point made by UK commentators was that paying taxes has become the most patriotic duty undertaken by the majority of the population.

> **'Paying taxes is a patriotic duty'**

Social Capital and a Sense of Place: Sustaining Vitality and Decencies

De Valera's images of the good society in 1943, 'a countryside bright with cosy homesteads', was suffused with a sense of place, but with the fatal flaw of no grasp of economic reality; it was an impossible ideal given the urbanisation policies and trends of the time, according to historian **John Joseph Lee**:

The most salient fact of Irish urbanisation since independence has been the growth of Dublin. This has been associated with the centralisation of government in Dublin, the disproportionate location of university places in Dublin and the concentration of job creation at the upper end of the scale in Dublin. Dublin largely plays the role of the metropolitan power towards the rest of the country. Dublin is overwhelmingly the media capital, serving in large measure as an enclave for imported thought.

It can be argued that the Ireland of today has little time for country or even towns. Towns as well as villages have been sucked into the Dublin vortex. It is defined in terms of the exclusion of those who fail to conform to the model of the geographically mobile, who have no need of a sense of place. People exist only as producers or consumers. There is only one generation involved, there being no place for the uneconomic. It is a one generational Ireland, it is an economy, not a society. The objective challenge of generational solidarity has become more daunting with the passage of time. With both parents in many cases working outside the home, the caring function, whether for the elderly or the young, has been increasingly transferred to institutions. Children and the elderly get in the way of economic man or woman.

A certain sense of place has an important role to play in sustaining the vitality and the decencies of civil society. This depends partly on the future of the family in Ireland, which is now increasingly contested. Much will involve how far families can provide secure moorings for the emotional stability of their members or how far they become one more institution to be functionally exploited, to be embraced or discarded as individual opportunism dictates.

The sense of place cannot survive without adaptation. Some of this follows inexorably from the changing nature of work. Farming has dwindled. The concept of a job for life is no way as pervasive now as before. Young people think nothing of changing jobs several times. It may be that developments in information technology will revolutionise the relationship between home and work, but this will not happen overnight.

'How does one reconcile rootless individualism with social solidarity?'

In an era of rapid change, and of more frequent questioning of identities, a sense of place has now to be cultivated. Given the pressure on families, even fairly close-knit ones, it is now institutions outside the family that bear much of the burden in providing bonding relationships. The psychic sense of place will become more important than simply a physical one, even though the physical will inform the psychic. The issue is how does one reconcile the principle of rootless individualism with a sense of social solidarity?

This is a profound challenge in an age of globalisation. What is globalisation? It is not a benign blending of all that is best of all the cultures in the world? Far from being a blending, it is an imposition of the strongest material and media culture on the weakest – a euphemism for Americanisation, or at least a segment of it. Ironically, a power whose greatness is built on diversity is now threatening to reduce the world to uniformity in the name of diversity.

The first requiem of a vigorous indigenous response is that there be sufficient worthwhile jobs at home to persuade young people to stay in Ireland, with prosperity throughout the country. The biggest hope for diffused prosperity is diffused third-level education. The location of economic activity is increasingly influenced by access to good quality higher education. One of the major challenges of regional educational institutions is to develop a capacity for independent critical thought, which will clinically evaluate media thought, whether metropolitan or directly imported. They have to be education centres, not indoctrination centres.

Parity of place has to be a core value of any democratic, pluralistic society. A sense of place implies belief in an inclusive society, where the weak are cherished as much as the strong. If Ireland is to become a genuinely inclusive pluralistic society, a balanced sense of place can make an important contribution.

Social Capital and the Workplace: Bringing Our 'Whole Selves' to Work

Why should we bother with the human dimension in the workplace? This was the question posed by **Catherine McGeachy**, then managing director of a company focused on effecting value change in individuals and organisations. McGeachy spoke of a survey that ranked human performance ahead of productivity and technology as a source of competitive strength:

The ability to attract and retain the best people is predicted to be the primary force influencing business strategy in the future. If you make your organisation a compelling place to work, it becomes a compelling place for customers and ultimately turns the organisation into a compelling place in which to invest. To make somewhere a compelling place to work, an organisation has to focus on its intellectual capital – its people. Intellectual capital is developed by making people competent and committed, and by allowing them to converge and operate as a team.

Research points to the building of community as a central 'gluing' agent. There are two ways in which a sense of community can be created in the workplace: building spirituality at work and removing fear from the workplace.

> *'Community can be created in the workplace by building spirituality at work and removing fear from the workplace'*

Why is there an interest in spirituality at work? People want to bring a greater sense of meaning and purpose into their work lives. They want their work to reflect their personal mission in life. Are spirituality and profitability mutually exclusive? Companies with a defined corporate commitment to ethical principles do better than companies that do not make ethics a key management component. How is spirituality manifesting in the workplace? More employers are encouraging spirituality as a way to boost loyalty and enhance morale. Growing numbers of business people want to bring their whole selves to work – body, mind and spirit. The means by which spirituality is manifest in the workplace is typically through three mechanisms: embodying personal values of honesty and integrity; treating employees in a responsible way; and making the organisation socially responsible.

The second way of building a sense of community in the workplace is by removing fear from the workplace. Negative dispositions can attract other negative dispositions. So individuals have to learn to take responsibility for their inner dispositions and the outcomes they were bringing to them. Thus our organisations should examine more thoroughly the quality of thinking taking place in their workplaces, and 'clean up' the thinking of their leaders and employees, helping them to think constructively. How can organisations remove fear from the workplace? The role of communications is critical – encourage feedback without repercussions; create a culture in which people are free to say what is on their mind; draw out different views of a situation; encourage appreciation of difference. Applying many views to a discussion and decision is central.

Another way of removing fear from the workplace is to check the 'disposition' of the organisation. Find out what employees are picturing in their minds – is it positive or negative? The pictures in our minds control our behaviour and control our level of motivation. Do employees feel they are part of a community that empowers them? Are employees aware that their thoughts affect their colleagues mentally and physically and the general working atmosphere? It is time we made individuals at all levels of the organisation responsible for the outcome of their thoughts.

> **'Find out what employees are picturing in their minds'**

The final way of removing fear from the workplace is by redesigning the organisation's appraisal system. We rarely measure a sense of community in appraisal systems. In Ireland, we have the living and successful experience of *meitheal* where people are naturally, culturally encoded to help their fellow man or woman, getting great results in the process. Yet we have cut across this, ignored it and the enormous gains it brings, and trained our people to be self-centred and to engage in unhealthy individualism. Intellectual capital is developed by helping employees to be competent, committed and team-driven. We must build the human dimension in the workplace.

Social Capital and Health: Care of the Sick is a Distinguishing Mark of a Society

Medical care is at the heart of social capital. At the centre of any health service is the patient. They require help and treatment, be it physical or mental. Their maladies may range from the trivial to the terminal, and the consequences of their illnesses may adversely affect others – family and indeed community at large, as in the case of communicable disease. The second focus of the service logically has to be on the caring professions – medical, nursing, and all the various paramedical disciplines, according to cardiac surgeon **Maurice Neligan**, who explained that:

These observations are obvious and would meet with little dissension. How, then, is it so difficult and contentious to conjoin the two groups to provide the best treatment and comfort for the sick and in so doing achieve the optimum conditions and stimulating environment for those entrusted with their care?

Amongst the distinguishing marks of a society is the care taken of the sick. How do we fare in this charge? In all honesty, we would have to say badly. It is true indeed that those accessing care usually find it to be of excellent quality. The access, however, may not be easy and can also depend upon ability to pay. Everybody rightly decries this as a criterion but, curiously, past political direction seems, far from ameliorating this socially iniquitous problem, to actually strengthen it further.

This country has four million people and is relatively wealthy. It should not be beyond our wisdom and knowledge to devise a system where the sick are treated expeditiously, effectively and with dignity, and that furthermore such should not be dependent upon the ability to pay. This should not be read as public is good and private is bad: the problems arise in the admixture.

Related to this, end-of-life caring in its wider social context had been raised by **Sinead Donnelly**, a consultant in palliative medicine, who reported that the team of carers must pay great attention to the detail of care both for the person who is very ill and to their family and friends:

In a way it is like helping to prepare a beautiful manuscript: the manuscript of the person's life as it comes to a close. We are, in fact, helping to prepare a script of a person's life at a critical time. We have to be interested in a holistic way in the individual who is suffering, not only their physical well-being but all the other components that create suffering – emotional, social, spiritual.

There is a lot to learn from looking to the past, for example the tradition and practice surrounding death and dying in Ireland. Looking at photographs of old funeral processions shows such dignity and respect, saying a lot about the mystery of death, its impact on the community and how the community can deal with its grief. People referred to death as a change – a transmutation – a change in substance. The language we use reflects our attitudes to change, to humanity, to life and to death.

'We have to be interested in a holistic way'

How can we capture the closeness of the spirit world, the sense of community, the acceptance of mystery that was part of our attitude to death and dying in the past? How can we take elements, the essence of that, and bring it into the present to create change and improve standards of care? There must be a way we can capture the richness of the past, moving it into the present, informing the present and improving care.

Social Capital and Policing: Trust and Alliances

In the criminal justice arena there has been an evolution towards community policing, according to **Kathleen O'Toole**, the first chief inspector of the Garda Síochána Inspectorate. In the past, police spent all their time on enforcement and 'fighting crime', but little on prevention and problem solving:

It was the police versus the community. But with rising crime levels, this approach was failing so the US started on a new paradigm: community policing. The approach was to reach out to community leaders in the most challenged districts who stepped up and rallied their neighbours in support of community policing. The police worked closely with these groups and with all the relevant authorities and private sector – not only to stop the wrong-doers and protect law-abiding people, but also to promote opportunities for kids on the edge, improve infrastructure and services, regenerate neighbourhoods and address quality of life issues.

Community policing became an ethos on which everything else in the police force was built. Every successful strategy was a holistic one, involving engaged and committed community members and partner organisations. The aim was building trust and alliances between police in the front line and those working and living in the communities. The essential strategy is 'Collaboration – Prevention – Intervention', and, when needed, relentless and effective enforcement. All of this must be built on a solid foundation of community policing and human rights. In Ireland, the good news is that the vast majority of Irish people still support the Garda Síochána and, in spite of past controversies, the Irish still stand firmly behind their police.

'A new paradigm: community policing'

Former Police Ombudsman for Northern Ireland **Nuala O'Loan** confirmed this:

Policing must be capable of operating locally. Communities with high levels of crime can become very dangerous places for those who live there and for those who seek to police them. There is now, in policing, a recognition of the importance of community policy to counter these risks. There are now highly developed mechanisms for community policing. Police must do all they can to ensure that local communities do not come to regard the police as their enemy. Community policing must develop before there is a problem in a particular area. Once the community is alienated it is very hard to undo the damage.

Community confidence thus demands accountability. Accountability is critical for delivering justice within society and the recognition of the need for accountability is the product of a mature state – one that can allow the examination of that which was done corruptly or criminally and that can be strengthened by the process of accountability, to become a stronger, more just state. The governance of states is a complex process and it inevitably involves the balancing of competing rights and freedoms.

In Ireland, we can identify instances of corruption: planning irregularities; criminal justice compromise; the corrupt power of wealth to subvert normal governance and in so doing to undermine the very principles of our state. There was a tendency in the governance not just of our state but also of our Church for those who exercised power to become overly conscious of the need to protect their power, and the opportunities for personal enrichment, which can result from the exercise of power. Here was a tendency too to exaggerate the need for secrecy and the protection of the governance processes. The characteristics and powers of the policing system must enable the delivery of an effective accountability process when they are exercised by those who themselves are aware of the danger of their own corruption, and of the need to act with total integrity. What matters is that the accountability process itself is open, transparent, impartial, accountable and evidence-based.

This social context of crime was highlighted also by RTÉ crime correspondent **Paul Reynolds**, who highlighted that although Ireland has a relatively low crime rate, there had been an increase in the numbers of murders and incidents of manslaughter in past years:

Since the 1970s, more and more people have been dying violently and arguably this generation is more violent than the previous one. What is perhaps more disturbing is not the increase in the figures but the increase in the level of violence associated with these crimes. Crime is becoming more violent and there are cases where people are attacked and beaten for the money in their wallet or their mobile phone.

If we are going to at least try to deal with the increase in violent crime, we have to ask ourselves why it is happening. If we can identify the reasons why, then we can identify the sources of the problem, thus leading some way towards finding a solution. The reasons are obvious and are so obvious they have now become clichés.

Population increase has concentrated more people in cities and expanding towns – focused locations of crime. Poverty is a factor, in that it is a well-documented fact that poor people are more likely to end up in trouble with the law and find themselves before the courts and locked up in jail. Studies have shown that the vast amount of prisoners come from a background and family life of considerable socio-economic and cultural deprivation. It is not just people from particular parts of the country but those from particular parts of our cities and towns who are most likely to become involved in crime. People living in disadvantaged areas with high levels of unemployment, social housing and few educational or recreational opportunities are more likely to be involved in crime. Education too is a key factor, with too many children leaving our educational system without having the basic tools of survival in our economy. For many children, the schools provide a refuge from the difficulties they experience living in dysfunctional homes in problem areas. Alcohol abuse is a critical factor, with Garda reports finding that 80 per cent of all crimes are rooted in drink. We see its effects on our streets every night of the week. Drugs are perhaps the most worrying of the major contributors to crime in Ireland, not just because of the damage they do to individuals, their families and their communities, and the craving addiction experienced that leads to horrific crimes, but also because of the associated increase in the availability of guns, which has made it easier for violent criminals to get hold of them. Criminal gangs have become a part of many areas.

Criminals such as these are not aliens, they did not come down from another planet. Many of these people did not get the same love, care or social and educational opportunities that the conventional population got. They did not get the same chance. They were marginalised and criminalised. The found their sense of belief, belonging, worth, livelihood and leisure in the criminal gang. And guns, drugs and violence are all part of that way of life. Tackling the causes of crime may be a truism, but if you tackle the problems of poverty, disadvantage, marginalisation and in particular the lack of education and opportunity, you could go a long way.

'Criminals are not aliens'

Conclusion

What comes across in this review of social capital is the massive agenda: so wide-ranging, yet all focused on the relationship between the individual and the larger community and centred on the ethic of care. This brings with it a potentially vast array of policy instruments and challenges. As such a policy framework, social capital thus provides a vital foundation for other actions, particularly in resourcing individuals within a positive setting of power and leadership. We now turn to these two issues.

Resourcing people has to be centre stage in any debate about values, but it brings with it immense challenges: How do we define it? What does it mean? What are the big issues? On whom should we focus? How do we do it? Bringing clarity to these topics is a substantial task.

THREE

Resourcing People

Resourcing People Through Reflection and Authenticity

Helping people to manage their future was one of the biggest challenges facing society, according to **John Drew**, visiting professor of European business management at Durham University, who spoke of the major opportunity in western civilisation to work on the reawakening of the inner dimension to our lives, which for many has withered or lain dormant:

This is very much about connecting our inner selves to our everyday lives, and the words we choose to do this are important. We place heavy emphasis on communicating, but less emphasis on the words we use when communicating. People are longing for more support and guidance as they feel their way hesitatingly towards a better understanding of their inner lives.

There is a growing and unfulfilled demand from many people in key positions in the world to reflect on and perhaps be guided on their personal development and search for an inner path. The first external path is where we tread on our sparrow's flight from the cradle to the grave. The second, or inner, path branches off it somewhere along the way and is discovered by some people at some stage in their lives.

Drew reported that what he was providing at business school was space for the participants to reflect not only on their business, but on the totality of their lives. Many managers were seeking to clear the foliage that blocked their view of the second or inner path. That foliage was perhaps the relentless pressure under which they were being put to achieve organisational success:

Looking to the future, there is a two-way pulling of our national roots – in one direction by steps towards world regional and global government – and in the other by demands from local communities and individuals for greater freedom of action. Just as our economic and societal arrangements are changing, so are we developing rapidly as individuals. We demand freedom, which also means choice. Since the earliest times, we have discovered our gods in animals, trees and rivers and our beliefs in the mysteries of the universe and the shadow side of our souls.

> **'The rebirth of a personal, sometimes spiritual, dimension in our lives'**

Since the eighteenth century, the widespread acceptance of critical thinking led to a gradual and partial revision of traditional religious attitudes. The effect has been to erode the influence of some traditional religions, leading to individual disappointment, disenchantment and dispossession. We are now witnessing the vacuum which this has brought about in the lives of individuals. It is being filled, however tentatively, by the rebirth of a personal, sometimes spiritual dimension in our lives. It is seemingly random and uncoordinated at this stage, but could lead to individuals attempting to better organise, direct and take responsibility for their own personal management and inner development.

How can we as individuals and managers respond to future challenges? Drew's view was that we should try to understand better the nature of change, to have some effect on the unfolding of events through studying the past, understanding the present and seeking a framework for understanding the future:

Perhaps we can work on closer integration of our economic, social and personal spheres. We must train to be on our toes, like a tennis player. Being aware and keeping ourselves mentally on our toes would give us a better chance of managing change. The cardinal virtues seem to play a bigger role in success stories than marketing and finance or planning and production, which seem to be more or less mechanical activities once the issue of creativity, innovation, moral responsibility and concern for people as individuals has been properly resolved. This reflects the growing need for personal development and space for individuals to reflect on the totality of their lives.

Following this theme of the inner-self, **Kieran McKeown**, a social and economic research consultant, reported that well-being has been measured using a very simple question: 'All things considered, how satisfied are you with your life as a whole these days?' He went on to explain its complexities:

Well-being includes life satisfaction with many domains including the thoughts, feelings and hopes about oneself and one's abilities, the family relationships with one's partner and one's children, and the broader social environment where one lives, including one's support networks, the quality of neighbourhood and access to services.

Overall well-being is a subjective state with three key dimensions. The first is personal well-being and is measured by life satisfaction, depression and hope (sometimes called locus of control). The second is relational well-being and is measured by the relationship with one's partner, one's child and the parent's perception of the child's difficulties. The third is environmental well-being and is measured by the availability of social supports, the existence of local problems in the neighbourhood (such as its appearance, safety, noise and litter) and access to local services (such as playgrounds, parks, sports facilities, schools, public transport and shops).

Three variables are dominant in influencing well-being: positive emotions, negative emotions and socio-economic status.

Positive and negative emotions are interdependent, not contradictory. Positive emotions are typically associated with an action-orientation geared towards pleasure and reward, and are regarded by psychologists as adaptive to procuring resources for survival. Negative emotions are typically associated with a withdrawal-orientation, geared towards avoiding pain and other undesirable consequences, and also regarded by psychologists as adaptive for survival by keeping us out of danger. Positive emotions have a positive influence on overall well-being, and negative emotions have a negative influence, so it is worth emphasising the importance of cultivating positive emotions. The good news about positive emotions is that they are not very dependent upon external circumstances – positive emotions have a more significant influence on overall well-being compared to economic resources.

'Positive emotions have a positive influence on overall well-being'

This means that a person's psychological resources (their habitual way of feeling and thinking) and their economic resources (their income and entitlements) combine to produce overall well-being. In other words, a person's well-being is shaped by their 'internal environment' (thoughts and feelings) and their 'external environment' (economic resources). Well-being can thus be traced to two core determinants – psychological resources and economic resources. Of these two, the evidence is that a person's psychological resources have a greater influence on well-being than the quantity of their economic resources. This suggests the need to recognise the importance of psychological resources in shaping well-being because of their crucial role in strengthening resilience to adversity. This also calls attention to the limit of economic resources in promoting well-being.

Thus psychological resources and economic resources are interconnected. A positive attitude helps to increase economic resources such as productivity and opportunities for promotion, while economic resources in turn improve positive emotions by creating opportunities for employment. Similarly, negative emotions can reduce economic resources by making a person less employable, or by weakening ambition and perception of opportunities.

This approach suggests that people who need help typically require either some psychological assistance in order to think and feel differently about their problems, or some practical assistance to overcome their economic resource difficulties – maybe even both. The key is that the well-being of individuals, their families and their communities is systematically interconnected. Well-being flows freely between the porous boundaries of the personal, the relational and the community. This underlines how intervention at any point is likely to have a ripple effect, as the process of cause and effect unfolds over time.

In this search for well-being, many people experience a great longing for authenticity, according to **Michael D. Higgins**:

We cannot live fully conscious lives unless we question the inevitabilities that are suggested to us. This involves developing the personal and social consciousness necessary to create a critical capacity so that we can truly experience freedom and choice and moral responsibility for the consequences of our actions. We will find no automatic solution in retreating to old certainties. This does not mean that the certainties should be discarded, only that they are insufficient. For example, policy frameworks around 'modernisation' and 'globalisation' are defective in that they are based on ideas that are unilinear, evolutionist and accepting of political and economic structures that are in political, economic and cultural terms dominating, exploitative and manipulative.

There is a need for questioning inevitabilities and certainties. But the way people handle this problem is escapist. People change beliefs and have done so in the history of ideas, through the construction of myths. The nature of a myth is that you suggest something is so obvious that it is natural for it to be taken for granted, like 'modernisation' and 'globalisation'. When we experience a longing for authenticity, consciousness tells us that spirit cries out for a version of the self and of the world, and for the capacity for creation that is not being met by our present circumstances. We have to answer the problem through an integrated scholarship that is not easily available to us anymore. We are all potentially creative, if allowed to develop. Accepting the necessity and power of creativity has implications for our economy. The creative society makes possible myriad forms of the knowledge economy.

One of the most important aspects of change in our contemporary lives has been the change in the relationship between economy and society. A new discourse has been invented to justify our subservience to the economy. Issues of personal and social development have given way to ones of utility. We are instructed on a daily basis as to what we must do with our lives to sustain the 'needs of the economy'. Our society is under pressure for time. Volunteerism is declining. There is little time for community. The relationship between the generations is fundamentally changing, with care of the elderly being almost exclusively discussed in terms of institutional provision.

> '**What is needed is a return to questioning the inevitabilities by which we live**'

A solution to our form of economy has to take into account the issues of income but also issues of quality of life. The challenge is to sustain the economy you desire, at the same time finding a way to realise our ethically unrealised selves.

What is needed is a return to questioning the inevitabilities by which we live, looking at some of the certainties discarded, critiquing the myths by which we live, concentrating on the critical capacity that the scholarship requires and that public debate requires, encouraging consciousness, respecting prophecies. The capacity to change our world still exists and we can create rather than remain the victims of history.

As an example of all this, simply listening was one of the greatest resources one could give to people, said **Alice Leahy**, director of homeless service TRUST. She explained how despite all the dramatic change we have witnessed, it is disturbing how undervalued human contact and genuine caring for others has become:

We may be rid of the workhouses, the orphanages and even the psychiatric hospitals, but, as one civil servant has said, this leaves prison as the last refuge for many of those vulnerable and unable to cope, whose difficulties are criminalised simply because there is nowhere else to send them.

'We need to make time to treat people as human beings'

We need to make time to treat people as human beings. This is the one thing that is increasingly difficult in the modern Ireland where we all seem to be statistics, reduced to a quantitative or monetary value. In a world increasingly governed by performance indicators and benchmarks, based on these quantitative measures is it possible to preserve even the concept of a philosophy of inclusivity, which means fundamentally treating people as people and as equals? The focus on people is being lost even as more resources are being deployed because it becomes almost impossible to advocate for a philosophy of inclusivity and caring when we distance ourselves from people. This distance is aided by technology: voicemails, emails and a flawed consultative process – all seemingly designed to keep people at a distance. But how can we ensure that people are treated as people? This is the most basic human right – the right to be treated as a human being and not as a statistic.

What those so far removed from the frontline in the development and planning of our health and social services fail to understand is that you cannot really listen to people without taking time to do so. Time is much more productive in the long term because by listening to people they will not become isolated, disillusioned or be made to feel worthless. Listening to people means we can help them avoid the misery of despair and exclusion in a 'democratic' society.

People in positions of power and influence should not allow jargon to take over and should be prepared to question rather than using reports to further distance themselves from people, or just support entrenched ideas that they already have. If they cannot or will not do that, a growing number will continue to suffer pain, often the pain of not being listened to, and those of us meeting with them are left with the feeling that we are only adding to their misery through our silence. Many people who work in community involvement are beginning to feel disenfranchised by an increasingly insensitive bureaucracy and meaningless jargon.

If we want a caring and respectful bureaucracy managing our health and social services, one that places respect for the dignity for every individual at the very centre of its operations, we now know that by adopting human rights-based management approaches we can achieve this. Caring for people as citizens does require us to speak out if we feel people are being denied care and liberty. If anyone is not being treated with dignity or, worse still, being excluded from society or our world, we have a big responsibility to be their voice. We also need to care for each other and defend those who speak out or nothing will change.

Resourcing People at Work: The Gift of Our Own Self-Worth

For people at work, here are critical issues: reduction of occupational stress, the need to realise the potential of employees, the role of the autonomous individual and the need to value diversity. In 1999, clinical psychologist **Miriam Moore** reported that, according to the World Health Organisation (WHO), emotional disorders stemming from work-related stress are among our most serious social problems:

Nearly every job is more stressful than it was before. Stress levels in the workplace, already rated as worryingly high, are predicted to get even higher. Organisations increasingly recognise that an emotionally balanced and satisfied workforce is the most important resource to keep the economic scales of business balanced in favour of success.

The evidence from the WHO was that work-related anxiety and depression were increasing. While stress can enhance performance, it can also be the kiss of death. Positive stress can turn negative when it is excessive or prolonged. This negative stress is what happens when we are losing our emotional balance. There has been an alarming increase in the extent of occupational stress. One of the most dangerous features of this stress is its cumulative nature, taking its toll on our personal lives, including our families and partners.

Major causes of occupational stress are several. There has been a revolution in the work environment, whereby firms and corporations are operating under huge pressure to survive and employees are treated as though they are dispensable commodities to be used up in the quest for profit. Overloaded, the world of work is becoming an overwhelming place of files and emails, leaving many employees with a great sense of time urgency and the need to work harder and longer. Change is often imposed or happens too quickly and employees can experience too much uncertainty and feel they are losing control. With fear and insecurity, employees afraid of being themselves tend to resort to passive-aggressive forms of communication, burying their real feelings while burning inside with resentment.

Overwork, fear, poor communication, enforced change, too much uncertainty, lack of emotional support and powerlessness are some of the salient factors contributing to stress. In addition, our social culture has been based on material success and acquisition. There has been a tendency to associate our happiness with having more. But richness is really a state of mind. A life without love and without people who care may be very rich in other things, but in human terms it is no life at all.

However, by changing our minds, we can change our lives. All is not well in the collective mind of the culture, but the conditions that cause us to lose our balance may also be the ones that present us with opportunities for psychological growth and learning.

> 'By changing our minds, we can change our lives'

We need to be aware of the values that we live by, for they have a profound effect on our personalities, our choices and our actions. Science is now telling us that nothing in the universe is separate. Everything and everyone is interconnected and interdependent, affecting and being affected by each other. A new value system has emerged, based on concepts of wholeness, relationship, respect for nature, for the feminine, for feelings and intuition and on the power of that mysterious Intelligence that radiates through our bodies and out into the universe.

There are a growing number of people whose attitudes are becoming more open, more tolerant, more authentic; people who are more spiritually and ecologically aware and who are searching for self-knowledge, simplicity and something more than the material, the measurable, the marketable. The more employers and employees are in alignment with this emerging paradigm of holism, relationship, inner power and self-worth, the more the workplace will become a place of maximum co-operation, trust, productivity and minimum stress. The best gift we can give to life, to work and to relationships is the gift of our own well-being and a sense of our own self-worth. The central responsibility for our inner harmony and balance lies ultimately with each of us individually. Self-knowledge, self-reverence and self-control are the keys to inner peace and balance.

Reflecting these issues, **Anne Coughlan**, a senior researcher with the Irish Business and Employers Confederation (IBEC), spoke of how the role of human resources in organisations had shifted somewhat away from issues of restructuring, downsizing and redundancies, towards how to realise the potential of employees:

Having 'your employees with you', and developing their unique potential, meant that the organisation stood a better chance in a globally competitive environment – in other words, employees could help companies gain a competitive edge.

There is a difference between 'family friendly' and 'work-life balance'. Family friendly policies tend to be focused on the needs of working mothers, while work-life strategies embrace the needs of different people at different stages of their life. It is often set within a broader diversity strategy, which recognises the needs of different groups of workers. The issue of work-life balance came about as organisations began to look at supporting the needs of their employees and not only working mothers with young children. It encompasses the notion of differences being valued and understood. It also holds that individuals at all stages of their lives work best when they are able to achieve an appropriate balance between work and all other aspects of their lives.

In businesses like these, the role of the resourced individual is crucial, according to writer, broadcaster and lecturer, **Charles Handy**, who predicted that the next problem of capitalism is the looming fragility, insecurity and frailty of our organisations, not just those in business, but in all our large organisations:

At the same time, and partly as a consequence, we are seeing the rise of the autonomous individual. This double happening is what is meant by the 'elephant and the flea'. This is a serious problem. These large organisations have been the pillars of our society. The last century was the century of the organisation – most people worked in them. But these 'elephants' are dramatically changing.

About 40 per cent of people who work for or with organisations work outside them. They are what can be called 'fleas' – small organisations, individuals, partnerships on some kind of contract arrangement, but not employed by the organisation. We can list the five types of fleas. First there are the 'in-house revolutionaries'. These are the mavericks. All organisations need these people and they need to give them space and allow them to experiment and, if need be, to be different from the norms. Then there are the professional and expert fleas – people who call themselves consultants, accountants and similar. Organisations are increasingly putting their best people outside because it is too expensive to keep them inside. Many organisations thus push their intellectual property outside and make them into these 'independent fleas'. Then there are the 'entrepreneurial fleas', people who create businesses and build organisations. There are the 'occasional fleas', the people at the beginning and the end of life, and finally there are the 'reluctant fleas', those who are pushed out of the elephant as redundant.

The dilemma for the elephants is the inexorable growth of competition, with demand for increasing productivity, and this means shedding fleas. But the elephants have another problem. Their assets are no longer in their buildings and their machines. Their assets are the heads and hearts of the people who work there. These people own the means of production in their heads and in their hearts, in their skills, their knowledge and their experience. They are very tricky assets to manage. They can walk away and be a flea.

As a 'flea', **Handy** reported that he had to work out his own purpose in life:

That becomes potentially very exciting. But the challenge for society is that lots of fleas are reluctant fleas. There are also incompetent fleas, ageing fleas and young fleas. These need help, to be transformed into independent or entrepreneurial fleas. We need to prepare people for fleadom in the real world. We need to teach people how to solve problems, how to sell yourself, how to find what talent you have and to make the most of it, how to turn it into a business or profession. We need a new system of words and heroes.

'We need a new system of words and heroes'

This role of the individual was echoed by **Orla Kelly**, organisational and effective manager at Hewlett Packard, who described how in many organisations there had been a movement away from the group focus:

In the 1970s and 1980s, the focus was on eliminating discrimination, righting the wrongs of the past and focusing on group membership. The focus has now been more on the individual. It looks at individual needs rather than the needs of people associated with particular groups. If we look at any group, for example, women or people with disabilities, we will see that not all people in the group are the same. They have different talents, different educations, different desires and different abilities. More and more, the focus in organisations has to be around valuing individuals and not necessarily focusing on the group. Group focus can be very useful, but it can be a very simplistic way of looking at diversity and can sometimes prove rather more exclusive than inclusive. As organisations move forward and learn more about this topic we will see more of a focus on the individual than on the group.

We are moving away from seeing diversity as a liability, or something that is to be tolerated, towards a place where diversity is seen as an asset. In the past, diversity was seen as something we had to live with, with people being expected to conform to the organisational culture that they were in, the dominant culture. Employees will no longer accept this. Employees want to be valued for their individuality. They will not accept being expected to conform.

There are visible ways in which people are different but there

'*Diversity is an asset*'

are also invisible ways. Age and gender are perfectly obvious ways in which you see someone as different to yourself. On the other hand, thinking styles is certainly a different one. So we need to look at the less obvious ways in which people are different.

Resourcing the Consumer: Expression of Choice is a Political Act

We live in an age of consumption. With steadily fewer people feeling the need to fight ideological wars, to protest or even to vote, it could be argued that the expression of consumer choice through economic transactions has become a defining political activity of our times, according to director of consumer affairs **Carmel Foley**:

Popular democracy, or the exercise of choice, is most often nowadays practised in the marketplace, not the polling booth. But in a marketplace, in exercising consumer choice, there can be a sharp imbalance between vendor and buyer. The dice can often be heavily loaded against the consumer. The buyer must still beware. So, we look to ways to tilt the balance back. We look for interventions, and these interventions can be personal, competitive or regulatory. The dominant ideological view in the EU is that effective competition is the best form of market regulation. But in an imperfect world competition is often imperfect, and not always effective – intervention, through regulation, will always be necessary. But even if we had the finest regulatory laws in the world, they will never truly meet their legislative and social aspirations unless people, consumers, are prepared to complain, to demand and to refuse. Consumer responsibility starts at the checkout, in what you might call a counter revolution.

Consumer protection legislation is terribly important. It sets standards, it protects, it creates a legal framework within which the consumer can get satisfaction or get their money back. Mostly it attempts to prevent problems before the business transaction takes place, with a legal fall-back when things go wrong. But the advice if you are faced with poor service or a faulty product, is to holler long and loud, and as embarrassingly as possible, until you get satisfaction. You are all well prepared to fight your corner in the marketplace.

'Holler long and loud, as embarrassingly as possible'

But sorting consumer problems is not just the responsibility of the legislation, or the aggrieved customer. It is primarily the responsibility of the service provider. Now some business people will see this as an additional burden in their haste to make a profit. But in these consumer conscious days, that attitude is a fast track to the bankruptcy courts. In response to this, the most progressive and successful businesses in the world are increasingly pursuing relationships with customers that are based on partnership rather than the adversarial model, of creating a sense of loyalty in their customers so that they become advocates rather than mere clients.

The concept of partnership in the relationship between business and consumer is a sophisticated and long-term view of the customer. This philosophy requires that instead of fearing the new sophisticated customer, businesses should view this sophistication as an opportunity. Pleasing a consumer is not an annoyance or an irritation. It is in fact a new and exciting way for companies to gain a sustainable advantage over their rivals. It's a new form of competition and a new form of consumer consciousness.

In Ireland, at an individual consumer level, there has been a great leap in confidence and consumer awareness. But there are still limitations. At an organised national level, popular organisations have been strangely quiet on the issue of consumer affairs. Community organisations, women's organisations, trade unions, or regional groups do not seem to see themselves as having a vested interest in consumer affairs. Ireland is different to many other European countries in that there is very little consumer activism at a community or organised level.

Also, 'acceptance by inertia' is another aspect of consumer/ provider relationships that causes concern. Vigilance is as important in consumer affairs as it is in other areas of public life. Our vigilance is being dulled by convenience. Our inertia then becomes something we pay for – literally in cash. Our inertia strips us of our critical responsibility to take charge of our affairs. The job of government is to provide the statutory framework of protection. The media can throw light on the problem. But in the first instance consumer relations emerge from a private contract between buyer and seller, an exchange of promise and trust. Both parties have the primary responsibility to make that relationship work. So let the buyer beware, and let the seller beware.

Resourcing Learners: What Sort of Models?

Resourcing learners needs to be done in many ways: by giving the right sorts of models to young people; by helping them to think things through for themselves and to learn through sport; by encouraging imagination and the value of tacit knowledge; through human contact in learning and by combating educational disparities.

Marie Murray asked what sort of models we offer our young people:

These models are in the images we allow them to see and those we protect them from viewing. We are alarmed at the apparent vacuum in the lives of young people and the manner in which many attempt to fill that vacuum.

The world of Irish adolescents changed radically in the closing decades of the twentieth century. What was once a traditional, single-race, agrarian, mono-religious, homogenous, economically impoverished, insular society became one of religious plurality, secularisation, liberal multiculturalism, economic prosperity, post-modern relativism, European identity and substantive technological traditions, particularly in adolescent means of communication and entertainment.

Entering into the adolescent arena is therefore a challenge for all who take any part in influencing the lives of young people, particularly when so many at this time are so disenfranchised, distressed, depressed, lonely and suicidal. A vacuum exists. Youth, at a time that should be full of hope, excitement and expectation, is instead filled with anxiety, depression and despair, illustrated by the stark statistics on suicide, crime, vandalism and drugs.

Analysis of what may make life seem vacuous and meaningless provides many potential contributory factors, not least the rapidity of societal changes at a speed that has traditionally been identified as causing the social malaise of anomie. This concept, developed by the French sociologist Émile Durkheim, describes a condition of deregulation: a state where people do not know what is expected of them nor what they might expect of others. It is a society without norms. It is a culture out of control, a culture with no standards of behaviour, no restraint on its activities. It is a culture that sounds much like our own.

In periods of rapid economic and social change, if traditional norms and standards are undermined, if new ones do not replace them, anomie exists and dissatisfaction, social deviance, disruption and violence increase. Allied to this is the demise of meaning by the removal of the moral order, provided by having religious beliefs. The loss of a belief system includes a loss of imagination in the most profound sense of the word.

'Give generously and love unconditionally'

Yet young people retain the reservoirs of idealism, energy and enthusiasm that have always characterised the young. They retain the capacity to give generously, love unconditionally and work strenuously for humankind. They can challenge critically, fight fairly, compete gloriously and battle bravely if we give them the inspiration to do so, the models to motivate them and the opportunities to be the best they can be. So we need to keep alive an ideology that interrogates the culture in which we live; to provide a vocabulary to discuss it and mechanism to confront it. Within this framework, the need is for a systemic approach to youth with clearly defined projects in sports, communication, connecting with nature, community networks, mental health and relating to the media.

This need for a systematic approach was also highlighted by president of the 21st Century Learning Initiative, **John Abbott**. He spoke of how we must regard every individual as 'being in the image of God' in order to elevate our relationships with another to the realms of the sacred:

Society is, however, fast losing that reverence for the 'specialness' of every individual. As humans, we are a confused species capable of great acts of altruism and the most terrible acts of cruelty. We are competitive as well as collaborative. Every moment of every day we have to make decisions, we have to discriminate between what we think is right and what, through natural law or perceived culture, we see as wrong. Such decisions are impossible to make without some sort of framework, a set of good stories if you like, that set the pace for individual choices within a culture.

So how are we educating the next generation to make good decisions, to steer our stone-age instincts through the intricacies of the early twenty-first century? 'Thinking things through for yourself' is a deeply ingrained human instinct, which generations of craftsmen have struggled to encourage. Inquisitiveness is one of the three or four key instincts that make possible our survival from generation to generation. The more you can think things through for yourself, the more in control of the future you become.

However, through the industrial revolution, society has been seduced by 'economies of scale' and in scientific management – telling people what to do rather than letting them work it out for themselves – society has greatly increased its material rewards at the cost of 'dumbing people down'. In contrast, the energy of adolescents, the experimentation with new ideas, is an essential part of the weaning of the individual's dependence on other people. It is also a key part of society's resources to deal with change. Adolescents come to adulthood through learning to balance correct reasoning with practical risk-taking skills.

Because our societies too frequently confuse information acquisition with education, we have overemphasised formal instruction and we have bypassed the individual

'Think things through for yourself' adolescent's deep-seated desire to think it out for himself. We need to give children an education that consciously gives them a progression of skills and attitudes which, as they grow older, will put them more in charge of their own learning and make them less dependent on teachers for instruction. This should release the deep-seated urge to 'do it for myself'.

As a practical example of people doing it for themselves, sport provides an enormous resource for good in our society, according to then chief executive of Sports Coach UK, **Pat Duffy**, who explained that sport has the potential to deliver many positive outcomes in terms of quality of life, personal fulfilment, health and well-being:

Sport puts us face to face with the outer limits of our potential more often than most activities. Sport also challenges us to face issues relating to right and wrong in pressurised and emotion-filled circumstances. Sport keeps us in touch with the importance of struggle and hard work. Western society has become increasingly sedentary, consumerist and complacent. Sport reminds us that to achieve anything of worth takes sacrifice, self-belief and teamwork. Sport also has the capacity to pull us out of the everyday comfort zone.

So, sport has the capability to move us into a realm that we have often forgotten about. But instead of sport being just a mirror of society, we should think of sport as a magic mirror, one that reflects society in all its facets but also one that can talk back: a mirror that takes on the mantle of leadership and moral courage, a mirror that reminds us that we have a soul and that without soul, sport and indeed living are just mere existences. For sport to fulfil this kind of transformative role it needs a clear vision of what it is about, and that is strong leadership guided by the right values.

Sport provides a unique way of giving people the opportunity of coming together and operating at community level. For example, the GAA and the FAI between them boast over 6,000 club units, mostly operating at local level. However, despite the huge contribution of this physical activity to Irish society, we have a policy and priority paradox – the place of physical education and sport is tenuous. In our primary and post-primary schools, the place of day-to-day physical education is languishing in a position that is probably at the bottom of the league in Europe. Despite the recent improvements in the curriculum, we are still in a position where our children are getting only one or two opportunities for physical education each week. Physical literacy is being neglected.

If we want our children to feel a sense of self-worth, they need a balance of what they receive from their parents and what they receive from the education system. We need to consider the joy of physical activity along with the joy of the arts, conversation and companionship. If we want to enhance the self-worth of our children, one of the most important things we can give them is the physical literacy skills that will enable them to feel capable and confident in their own bodies. For we all live, breathe and feel through our bodies and it is through the fusion of spirit, mind and body that human potential and quality of life can be truly maximised.

> 'It is through the fusion of spirit, mind and body that human potential can be maximised'

Sport has tremendous potential to be a transformative force in Irish society. Through sport we can commit to building fair and open pathways for our children, thus providing healthy experiences for them that enhance their self-worth and integrate their lives more strongly with family and community.

Broadcaster **Mike Cooley** envisaged a future for young people where the capacity to identify and build on the positive features of technology would be developed and its negative features marginalised:

Technological change is usually portrayed as a universal good and a 'win-win' situation. In consequence, we often fail to deal with, or even consider, its multiplier effects and how best to cope with these. The rate of change is bewildering. The idea that schools and universities can provide young people with a tool-kit of knowledge and competence to use it for the rest of their lives is obviously no longer valid. Rather, we should encourage our young people to retain a child-like curiosity, a learning habit and a sense of the mysterious. We have become far too smart scientifically to survive much longer without wisdom. We need to develop a symbiosis between machines and people, a symbiosis to design systems that support, enhance and celebrate human intelligence. The most precious asset any society, country or culture has is the skill, ingenuity and imagination of its people.

The future for our young people should be one in which their capacity to judge and imagine will be encouraged and treasured. As matters stand, our society is moving in the opposite direction and there is a drastic shift from judgement to calculation. We are told we are in an information society and are now becoming a knowledge society, but such a theory should be questioned. We are certainly in a data society. Transforming data into information is a meaningful human activity. Applying this information turns it into knowledge which, when absorbed into culture, can result in wisdom leading to appropriate action. At the knowledge/wisdom/ action end we find 'tacit knowledge'. These are the things we know but cannot tell. Tacit knowledge incorporates the sense of size, shape, form and appropriateness that comes from working in the real world around us. Our educational system continues to overemphasis the significance of data ('facts') that have not been tempered by a process of experience. We are losing our ability to judge and are increasingly reliant on calculation.

'We are losing our capacity to judge'

We need 'human-centred systems' with tools to support and enhance human skill and ingenuity rather than replacing them by calculation alone. So often, the big issues in society and in science and technology are prefigured by culture, music, literature and poetry. In the future, these forms should be treasured and respected as highly among young people as the abilities in science and technology. Furthermore, it should be a future in which we respect a whole variety of learning abilities and individual learning styles, one in which there will be a possible symbiosis of the formal and the informal, the explicit and the implicit.

In most instances, students travel though a rather conventional education system from secondary school and onto university, graduating without much practice into the work place. Conversely there are those who gain their knowledge through informal learning and acquired implicit knowledge. People acquire their abilities in all sorts of diverse and unorthodox ways. Critical in all these matters is motivation and how motivation is stimulated by imagination. If you are highly motivated and adults support and encourage you, it is quite extraordinary where it will lead. Truly motivated people have an extraordinary way of marshalling capabilities and reserves of skill to undertake something. The education system generally ignores the importance of intentionality and purpose, all of which lay the basis for that extraordinary human attribute – transcendence. This is the ability to recognise mechanism and processes that allow us to go beyond the present state of things.

It is always constructive to try to emphasise what people do know rather than what they do not know, and to consider what motivates them so we can build on that. However, in many cases our system tends to do the opposite. We are relying more and more on rule-based systems. These are held out as a sort of panacea in large corporations, local government, health care and in schools.

But we have to valorise diversity. It would be sad if, now that we are beginning to understand the significance of biodiversity, we were to ignore the significance of cultural and linguistic diversity and, for example, succumb to the cultural imperialism of technocratic jargon. We have to be able to imagine what we might want and what we might be. Our young people should be encouraged – even provoked – into embarking on that journey of imagination.

This idea of tacit knowledge was also taken up by writer and former broadcaster **John Quinn**. Reporting that schooling accounts for only 20 per cent of a young person's life, what, Quinn asks, fills and influences the other 80 per cent?

Today's society demands curiosity, initiative, collaboration and adaptability from our school leavers. Contrast that with the annual paranoia on what comes up in the leaving certificate. But in the real world what comes up is life, with all its delights, disappointments, cruelties, vicissitudes. Beyond the walls of school, beyond the chains of certification, beyond the prison of professionalism there is an awful lot of tacit knowledge – the things we know but cannot tell, and cannot be written down or explicitly stated. It takes a village to raise a child, but what has happened to the village and where is the child? Once there was community, time and no technology. Now we have little community, no time and all the technology. Community is under siege. The people are still there, more and more of them at an older age, a whole army of retired people with talent, wisdom, experience and time. We need a nationwide 'sharing our skills', where tacit knowledge is freely shared in a community. It would be a way of rebuilding, refocusing community.

Children are biological beings, not machines. They need time to grow and develop, time to reflect, play, interact. Instead we hurry them. As they grow older, the pace increases when in fact they need the 'gift of the interval'. Young people need to acquire the habit of reflection because they will not pick up the habit in later life. Rather, in later life there will be a sense of opportunities lost, of dis-ease. We need to take a long hard look at what we are doing to children and childhood. Children need life to be real. They need real food, real play and real adults – not junk food, sedentary screen-based entertainment and absent adults. They need time and protection from stress.

Our schooling, dictated by examinations, is heavily left-brain-oriented, the logical, linear cause and effect – is there a book on it? What's the answer? To the exclusion of the right brain – what if? Supposing that ... how did that happen? We are besotted with seeking the 'right answer' when often there is no right answer.

We must take into account modern research in the way we learn – the role of technology in independent learning; the recognition that adolescents are capable of taking responsibility for much of their own learning – with tutoring rather than 'teaching' from adults; the recognition of multiple intelligences; the possibilities of intergenerational learning; of learning beyond the walls of a classroom; and that education is a lifelong process.

'We need to foster curiosity and collaboration in our young people'

To make this happen there needs to be real innovation in the curriculum and the organisation of learning. We need to foster curiosity and collaboration in our young people and a spirit of inquiry and possibility. We need to open the doors of our schools for a two-way flow of traffic – elders, mentors, volunteers inwards and students outwards into the community. We need to slow down, to give ourselves and our children time.

Expanding on this need for a 'flow of traffic', the importance of connectedness and human contact, **Catherine Byrne**, former general treasurer and deputy general secretary of the Irish National Teachers' Organisation (INTO), emphasised that life is about contact – physical, social, emotional and intellectual. The opposite is to be disconnected, alienated, isolated:

The OECD have said that we are moving into the 'knowledge economy', where the success of individuals, firms, regions and countries will reflect, more than anything, their ability to learn. In the knowledge society, schools should be the key knowledge organisations, centres of excellence for learning where curiosity, creativity, innovation, risk-taking and life-long learning are nurtured and encouraged. This should be our aim, not primarily because our economy needs it in order to compete effectively, but because children and adults need it to fulfil their potential, to live meaningful lives and to participate fully in the social, economic and cultural life of their community and society.

The school of the future will continue the current trend of transforming schools from a collection of individual classrooms into a community of learners with teams of teachers who are interdependent and equal contributors to the life of their school and the progress of their pupils. The school of the future will have a holistic approach to the student, recognising the child as an individual with a multiplicity of needs – physical, emotional, intellectual, spiritual, social. Human beings are complex, and in the past we have perhaps failed to fully appreciate this in educational terms. We have perhaps concentrated on knowledge and a narrow understanding of intelligence. In this fast-moving world our young people must emerge from their years in the classroom as well-rounded, confident members of society, not just accomplished products with economic value for the employment market.

> **'Schools should be communities of learners'**

The school of the future needs to recognise and appreciate that there are multiple intelligences. The most important thing we can give a young person is the confidence to be themselves. If they are secure and feel valued for who they are, they will emerge as people connected with themselves and will not need targets for their own lack of self-worth, anger and fear. Not being connected means being alienated.

Connecting with all learners was highlighted by **Mary Forde**, former principal of Presentation College, Athenry. Forde spoke of how there continued to be a significant disparity between the educational attainment of those from higher socio-economic backgrounds and those from less-advantaged homes and backgrounds:

A number of factors contribute to the capability of children and young people to engage in learning and to make the most of their educational opportunities. These include being able to make good choices and decisions; an understanding of the impact of their actions – 'If I do this, predictably and consistently that will happen' – and how to influence events; and the ability (and desire) to concentrate, to apply themselves to a task and persevere.

Reports highlight evidence that some children are less likely to have access to experiences that help them to develop these skills and attitudes. Consequently, while activities to promote such development are of value to all children and young people, they are of particular value to certain groups in closing the attainment gap. These skills and attitudes are as important in further and higher education as in the workplace. However, the national curriculum gives them relatively little weight and they are measured, recorded and reported inadequately by national tests and most public examinations. As a result, they are in danger of being neglected by teachers and undervalued by pupils and their parents at a time when they matter more than ever.

'Being able to make good choices and decisions'

Some schools are already succeeding in narrowing the gap. They are achieving very different outcomes for their pupils, compared with other schools with similar pupil profiles. A strategy for closing the gap through personalising learning and creating a caring environment through care teams will draw heavily on solutions adopted in schools where pupils buck the trend.

Resourcing the Family: The Future Well-Being of Children

We need to place greater emphasis on family support, reported **Geoffrey Shannon**, solicitor and senior lecturer in Family and Child law:

Family support services play a vital role in contributing to the future well-being of children and families. We need to invest in services where people can learn about relationships and parenting skills. We need greater investment in systems and supports for marriage and relationships. We need to support those marriages that are capable of being saved. We need to enable those that cannot be saved to be dissolved with the minimum of avoidable distress, bitterness and hostility. In short, we need to minimise the bitterness and distress engendered by the divorce process. We need to encourage, so far as possible, the amicable resolution of practical issues relating to the couple's home, finance and children and the proper discharge of their responsibilities to one another and to their children. We should seek to minimise the harm that the children of the family may suffer, both at the time of the divorce and in the future, and to promote, so far as possible, the continued sharing of parental responsibility for them.

Divorce disputes need alternative forms of dispute resolution other than the courts, although it must be said that the courts are needed for cases that cannot be resolved in any other manner. Alternative dispute resolution mechanisms at least aspire to promote consensus rather than conflict, which is particularly important for the welfare and dignity of the children, the subjects of divorce proceedings.

In addition, with regard to more comfortable, convenient and client-friendly court facilities, both the courts and parties to a divorce would benefit greatly from the promotion and more widespread use of mediation, collaborative law and other forms of alternative dispute resolution. This should be realised through more robust legislation facilitating alternative dispute resolution, which would minimise the number of contested cases ending up in the courts, and also reduce the level of 'brinkmanship' that sees many settlements being reached on the steps of the courts.

Such modern pressures on the family were also highlighted by psychologist, educator and author **John Yzaguirre**, who addressed the dramatic changes in family life in recent decades:

Studies on marital happiness show that in the last decades there has been a decline in marital happiness, less marital interaction, more marital conflict and more work-related stress. In the midst of the critical changes in family life, a significant search for greater emotional connection and intimacy is emerging. Couples are seeking a new vision on how to achieve lasting and mutually rewarding relationships. The good news is that couples can learn skills and acquire values with benefits that persist over time. There are three skill sets in the dynamics of family unity: empathy, autonomy and mutuality. Empathy skills involve learning to accept others as they are, to understand their needs, to love them concretely as they want to be loved. Autonomy skills are understood as developing a healthy self that does not ignore, dominate or submit to others, but relates to others in a co-operative and egalitarian way. Empathy and autonomy are necessary to achieve mutuality, but they are not sufficient. Mutuality requires interactive skills that aim at building and strengthening relationships and restoring them when needs be. The essential skills of mutuality include conflict-free communications, integrating personal differences and restoring unity.

'Search for greater emotional connection and intimacy'

Given the prevailing socio-cultural trends that weakened marriages and families, we need to promote healthy marriages and strong families in all levels of society by expanding educational and support programmes. The empirical evidence of marriage education programmes indicate that they are both well received and have generally positive and lasting outcomes.

The impact on the family of the changing nature of work was considered by **Charles Handy**, who spoke of how work has always structured the way we live:

Looking back to the agricultural economy, everything happened around the home and everybody stayed at home, in a sense. However, then came the Industrial Revolution and work moved away from the home and people went out to work. Offices replaced factories and the assumption was that you had to have all the people in the same place at the same time to get the work done. You had to move from the home to work, and that actually took the work out of the home.

Nowadays, more people spend at least part of their time in the knowledge economy or the information age: processing data, information, images and so on – this can be done anywhere. We are nomads, Bedouins; we carry our work with us. You can work anywhere you like: on an airplane, on the train, on a bus, or at home. Increasingly, people spend one or more days working from home if their bosses allow it, and their bosses could do well to allow it, because corralling employees, bringing them into the place of work, is incredibly expensive. Buildings cost money and, if you think about it, buildings are empty for two-thirds of the time. Therefore, the more people you can push out of the building to somewhere else and bring them in only for necessary meetings, the cheaper it will be – and the more liberating it will be. Of course, you have to trust people to work when they're out of your sight, and that's not easy.

What is interesting is the effect all this has on the family once you bring people back into the home. Most children now have some image of what work really means, as they see one or other of their parents working. The home is the really important classroom in life. Schools teach children useful things but it is in the home they learn the important things. That is where young people learn self-discipline, consideration for others, the limits to decent behaviour, and they learn what is right and wrong. Of course, you could also learn horrible lessons if you belonged to a bad family. But in a good family you learn the really important things in life and one of these is work: the discipline of work, the accountability of work, the responsibility of work. How else do you learn about it unless you see someone doing it? In the funny schoolroom that is the family, you do not have people preaching to you or teaching you or lecturing to you most of the time. You learn by watching; it is a sort of unconscious, subliminal schoolroom.

'The home is the classroom in life'

Thus, the way the world is changing is actually bringing families back together in a funny way, because work if coming home again into the family. Furthermore, technology can bond people together, even if they are not able to put their children into the same kind of building. Instead of meeting children in the garden, they can meet them in cyberspace. Technology in a strange way is allowing people to be individual yet together.

Conclusion

The definitional challenges of resourcing people are still there, but perhaps the clarity is growing, focused around objectives of personal reflection, authenticity and human contact. And just like social capital, the potential number of policy instruments is myriad. But these can only be pursued in the context of supportive power and leadership, which will be considered in the next chapter.

FOUR

Power and Leadership

We need a diversified economic model, with emphasis on quality and adaptability, but well founded on the realities of globalisation, and promoting a shift towards a more egalitarian society.

The Need for Vision and Leadership: Adaptability and Quality
The flawed economic ideology of quantity over quality controlled and directed Irish economic and social policy from 1997 to 2008, according to **Jim Power**:

In the midst of such an unprecedented economic crisis, it is hard to see where an economic recovery could possibly come from and there is a strong temptation to plunge into the depths of despair, but that is not in the nature of the human spirit. There are still many individuals and companies operating in the Irish economy who believe in the future of the country and who will continue to try to make it happen. The challenge for policy makers is to create an environment where such individuals and companies are facilitated to the greatest extent possible in order to create economic activity and employment, and help Ireland realise its economic potential once again. Recovery is possible, and we have the 1980s to remind us of that.

In the 1980s, there was also little belief in the ability of the political firmament to extricate the economy from the mess it was in. It was through a combination of luck, sensible policy-making and, most importantly, strong political leadership that the economy managed to lift itself out of its difficult situation. For Ireland to emerge from the current economic malaise, a number of things need to happen: the global economic cycle has to improve; the crisis in the banking sector needs to be sorted out; the economy should become more competitive; the structure of the public finance system must be re-engineered to make it more sustainable in the longer term and better able to cope with future shocks; the damaged reputation of Ireland has to be repaired; and an economic plan needs to be put in place, identifying the sectors that can contribute to Ireland's economic future. The global and European economic situation is obviously outside Ireland's control, but the others are well within our own remit and must be tackled as a matter of urgent priority. In the context of competitiveness, we simply need to reduce the whole cost base of the Irish economy from wages, to local authority charges, to commercial rates and rents, professional fees and much more besides.

In the recent past, successive governments were prepared to ride the construction boom for all it was worth and grow the public sector as if it were the highest value-added sector in the economy. There was no real attempt made to develop other sectors of the economy to ensure that we had a diversified and sustainable economic model.

> **'It is incumbent on Ireland's policy-makers to plan for a more diversified economic offering'**

It is now incumbent on Ireland's policy makers to plan for a more diversified economic offering. This strategy has to involve a number of economic sectors in which Ireland can actually compete, ensuring that, insofar as possible, an environment is created whereby those sectors can develop. The economic plan for Ireland will have to combine the modern with the traditional, the old with the new and the indigenous with the foreign-owned. It is not a case of either/or, but rather some of both.

The mainly foreign-owned IT and chemical and pharmaceutical industries will remain important, but we will also need to develop sectors such as tourism, agri-food, alternative energy, the arts (one of the few industries in which Ireland is top-class) and the thoroughbred industry. We have to create a diversified economic model, based on quality and sustainability, and driven by a strategic and strong leadership.

This need for diversity was echoed by a call for adaptability and dynamism from economist and strategist **David McWilliams**, who looked at how history tells us that invention is not enough; it must be harnessed via the dissemination of information:

If countries want to get rich, inventions and their use must be passed down through the population. Therefore, lesson number one is that adaptability to new ideas and a level of economic freedom make it worthwhile to adopt new technologies. But societies can often go into reverse. This stemmed from a lack of dispassionate enquiry and a failure to oppose dogma. Dogma leads to economic stagnation. Lesson number two is that a society will remain dynamic if it allows dissent. It is no surprise that contemporary dictatorships tend to come unstuck due to economic underperformance. There seems to be a direct linear connection between questioning by the private individual (whether religious or otherwise), property rights and economic wealth.

Lesson number three is that size is not everything. A small dynamic country making the most of its talents and infusing its workforce with new ideas will outflank the competition. Size is not important and small may not only be beautiful but profitable too. Because harnessing ideas can be more important than innovation itself, countries can, contrary to popular belief, plagiarise their way to wealth. The crucial point is embracing technological change and not

> '*A small dynamic country making the most of its talents and infusing its workforce with new ideas will outflank the competition*'

being afraid to recognise when certain industries have had their day and it is time to move on.

The American example tells us that the keys to economic growth are people, property rights and relative intellectual freedom. If people are robbed of their economic freedom, they will become docile; likewise, a country with economic freedom but without people will simply run out of steam.

While the lessons of history tell us that the key condition is freedom, both intellectual and economic, they also suggest that economic development occurs in phases. At each phase, more adaptable, flexible people come in and add something special that renders their products more sought after than their neighbour's. The economic cycle that sees countries going from one phase to another is either accelerated or retarded by the general politico-economic environment prevailing in the country over several decades. Economic history is so littered by boom to bust stories that it is difficult to know where to start. When punters begin to pay over the odds for a certain type of asset, this triggers a boom to bust cycle. Economic history tells us both how economies succeed and how hubris can trip up even the most successful of these. Busts almost always follow booms.

The causes of the economic collapse were rooted in failures of political leadership, according to **Dearbhail McDonald**, legal editor at the *Irish Independent*. McDonald argued that we experienced a crisis for our democracy following an absolute failure of political leadership:

Why did it fail? The answers are myriad and complex. The economic collapse is a major factor, so too the shady relationships between politicians, banks, developers and other power brokers. The light shone on political corruption through our tribunals, the scandalous failure to regulate our banks, and controversies about expenses and waste of taxpayers' money. Abuse of public power for private gain, the cult of the individual and self-interest that permeated the whole of Irish society were also to blame.

We got lost and it is time to retrace our steps. In doing so, hopefully we will reach some sense of catharsis that will allow us to draw a line underneath this turmoil; allow us to embark on a more introspective journey where we ask deeper questions about leadership and personal responsibility. Leadership is not the preserve of those who, by accident or design, hold leadership positions. We are all called to be leaders and we all have the duty to participate in the decisions that affect our lives.

Is it right to outsource our personal responsibility to an institution in the first place? We need to build an alternative leadership concept around the leadership of service. Who is a leader? We all are. Whether we are running a country or a soup kitchen, we all have the ability to demonstrate leadership by seeking service over self-interest, by leading by example. The hairdresser who volunteers her time to pampering and building the self-esteem of those in our hospitals and hospices, is she not a leader? The bin men who clean our streets and preserve some semblance of environmental order, are they not selfless public servants? We all have a duty to act as custodians, to remember that what we have is not ours but a legacy, something that we hold on to for others, for future generations. The good news is that this type of selfless leadership is something that we Irish people excel at, even and especially when resources are scarce.

What is it about true leaders that we most admire? True leaders have a selfless devotion to public duty in that classic sense of the phrase. They have vision and the ability to give practical expression to that vision. We need a far-reaching vision of the sort of society we want to be when this crisis passes. We need to have courage and look beyond our immediate and pressing fears, to look within ourselves instead of seeking intellectual and financial

'We need a far-reaching vision of the sort of society we want to be when this crisis passes'

bailouts elsewhere. A new vision for yet another new Ireland would be a very good place to start.

Such new visions mean getting back to the truth, according to **Ged Pierse**, a leading figure in Irish commercial and sporting life, who urged that we harness the truth to give effect to change:

Our problems are not entirely home-grown. The truth is there has been a steep decline in standards across the western world. The collapse of major companies has been a wake-up call for the professionals to sort out their business ethics and to pull back from the rampant materialism and greed structures that have driven the American system in the past twenty years.

The reality of change in the corporate world is that the fundamentals never change. The integrity of the entire system is based on trust. The two professions that bear the greatest responsibility in this respect are the accountancy/audit and the legal profession. When these professions are more concerned with the quality of their fees than with the quality of their governance, the whole fabric of the system is threatened. The public have lost confidence in the legal profession in Ireland and they do not trust our accountancy bodies, our banks and our financial institutions. Our politicians have lost the trust of the voters, as evidenced by declining polls in elections, symptomatic of the lack of trust and apathy towards authority. We have suffered from weak government in this country for a number of years. The concentration has been on political survival rather than on proper government; on the cult and myth of personality instead of proper policies and actions.

But to be viable, visions must continuously change, reported then MD of Aer Arann, **Pádraig Ó Céidigh:**

Can you see the vision changing? Avoid getting stuck in the mud with the same vision. Move on. Some big companies are so inflexible about their vision. Vision changes, because life changes. Your vision now is different to what it was five years ago, and it will be different in five years time. Let it change. Allow it to change. Support it to change. If you are pushing a ball up a hill there will be days when it is raining and you slip back and the ball slips back too. There are days when you can push a little further. But as you push it up a bit, you know what happens – you start to get people in to help you push it up the hill. You get a little support and it gets easier. Sometimes there are little pebbles and sometimes big rocks in your way. They put you back a little bit but you manage to weave around them or even push the ball up over those rocks. Most businesses fail because they give up too early.

However, an overall national loss of vision has been a fundamental problem, said economist **Jim Power**:

There are some key challenges that we need to address. One would be the breakdown of authority, the problem of random violence on the streets, and the huge dependence on alcohol and drugs that has emerged. These problems are ones that the older generation has to take responsibility for. The whole culture of alcohol dependency in this country is directly feeding into a serious drugs problem. This is leading to a breakdown of authority, and poses a serious threat to the future stability of this country.

The leadership in this country has failed us badly: the authority of the Church has been seriously undermined, the authority of the political elite has been seriously undermined and the authority of the business elite has been seriously undermined. If you take out these three pillars that we all respected in the past, you are left with a vacuum and the question is: How do we fill that vacuum? How do we re-establish leadership, authority and, most importantly, respect for property and people?

The provision of public services is a serious issue, particularly health and education. Problems are primarily due to a lack of finance, but there is also a serious issue of mismanagement. We have to address these issues. How are we going to finance the provision of public services and how are we going to manage them?

Vision and leadership are not just issues for government, they are urgent issues for organisations and corporations too, according to **Stephen Covey**, co-founder of management and leadership development organisation Franklin Covey:

When we begin to experience the profound, constant and ongoing change, largely driven by the globalisation of technology, in the globalisation of markets, everything is affected by it. It is so easy to become a victim of it all and to lose a sense of control. We remember as we go back in history. As we shifted from one historical period to another, everything changed. This is going to happen in the future faster and more profoundly than most of us even imagine.

People want to have balance in their lives. They do not want to neglect their families or to see community life and the life around the traditional neighbourhood, the parish, community and family deteriorate. But the new reality has come upon them and it is very powerful and extremely seductive. Unless people take control of the situation and manage their response and manage their future, what will happen is that this balance in life and community/family aspects will become sicker and might even die.

Covey reported that in the United States the community and strength of the family had started to suffer a horrendous loss:

Also, corporations become so short-term focused that the short-term bottom line tends to dominate almost everything. This kills the trust inside organisations. It brings a profound form of disempowerment, with a neglect of energy, talent and resourcefulness.

Organisations are like the tree and the roots. The roots are the character, based on principle, and the tree is the personality, based on technology. While the tree comes from the roots, there has been a separation between character and personality and that has created a tremendous amount of trust issues inside communities and inside organisations. This has hurt the balance in people's lives.

For organisations to continue to lead, we need to deal with these kinds of problems: family, schools, community and safety in the streets. It is hard to attract people to communities that are not safe, to schools that do not have good solid cultures. Inside our organisations, we need to take a balanced score card approach, so that we are not just looking at the financial bottom line, we are also looking at what's happening to our people and what is happening to their families.

In Ireland, what **Covey** admired most was the authenticity, the genuineness of the people and the fact that relationship mattered more than things.

They were not just into efficiency, they were into effectiveness. That is, going for the results that really matter. This was so deeply inbred into the psyche and the intergenerational culture of this country that it was enormously attractive.

Organisations must focus on what is really important in the longer term, not the so-called 'urgent' short-term things that attract too much attention. Quality is the important thing and we know from surveys what is holding back quality. The number one issue is low trust. There is misalignment of structures and

> **'Organisations must focus on what is really important in the longer term'**

systems in organisations that nurture trust. Organisations say they value co-operation but in fact they reward competition, internally. They say they value the balance between short and long term but in fact they reward short term.

The net effect of the organisationally misaligned situation is that it causes the organisation itself to become misaligned with the marketplace business. Organisations are governed by the cultural rules of the workplace. If there is a low trust culture, this organisation or society will not be able to compete successfully in a global economy. You need a deep commitment from people and their culture to make things happen in the market.

We need leadership for the important things: modelling trustworthiness, path-finding future visions, aligning the values, empowering people. This can be done on a community basis. We have to work on both social norms and laws, to nurture the climate so that you have empowerment. We need vision, and to have the discipline and institutionalisation of that vision is the foundation that releases human potential. The vast potential of people is still undeveloped. How can that be realised? Only when people have a common criterion and then they are given freedom with guidelines to do whatever it takes to accomplish that criterion, to accomplish the goal.

Responding to the Challenge of Globalisation: Reform and Rethink
Globalisation blurs the distinction between global and local and introduces global competition into what were heretofore largely local allegiances. We thus need to reframe economic policy in ways that make us think not only about our own self-interest but of global self-interest. The big issue is about the reform of the corporate and institutional sector in the context of globalisation of the world economy. Engaging in such a New World Order implies collective responsibility. But properly grasped, globalisation

can bring many benefits so we must be agile; we cannot afford inertia. With continued globalisation, the issue of values is even more pressing.

Feelings of betrayal and the process of globalisation were dominant, according to **Tom Collins**, director of the Centre for Adult and Community Education at NUI Maynooth. He reported that change in Ireland was summed up by the phenomenon of having to turn our attention from problems that we have become accustomed to trying to solve, to problems that we have no experience of trying to solve. This raised interesting challenges: Ireland has been characterised by deep generational shifts, whereby the trajectory of the preceding generation is turned on its head, and a new trajectory emerges, with two major themes – democracy and development.

There were two key forces driving the redefinition of democracy in modern Ireland. One was the experience of betrayal and the other was the process of globalisation.

We have had the betrayal of a younger generation by an older generation. The many scandals that have plagued Ireland are effectively the betrayal of the present generation by the preceding generation. This calls attention to the civic nature of morality. We as a society must learn and develop from these events in terms of how we relate to authority and leadership. This path of reconstruction as a society must begin with unbelief rather than belief. This is the challenge of scepticism – a healthy negativity which requires that trust must be earned rather than conferred.

'*We have had the betrayal of a younger generation by an older generation*' This is not necessarily a negative starting-out position. The life cycle is a series of progressive learning challenges. This is surely the great value of history. The foundation of the Irish state merely replaced one overlord with another one – the Catholic Church replaced the colonial state. Religious adherence did not emerge from the ground up, but was imposed in much the same way as many of our colonial impositions. But we are now in a process of moving out of this phase in our history – into a post-clericalised period in modern Irish history. What will that mean for finding democracy?

Globalisation as a process is central to the emerging nature of democracy. Globalisation blurs the distinction between global and local and introduces global competition into what were heretofore largely local allegiances. This involves the 'interrogation of tradition' where we re-work our culture in exciting and new ways, rather than habitual acceptance. This also means a new 'basis of solidarity', where relationships are a matter of choice rather than legacy. Trust is thus earned rather than conferred, and this underpins new notions of governance, with more emphasis on participatory democracy.

The second major theme is the development challenge. We have no history to guide us on how to handle the next ten years. Erich Fromm distinguished between a state of 'having' and a state of 'being'. A state of 'having' is a condition whereby self-worth is based on the appurtenances of a consumer age. Attributes that are external to the person assume a core significance in the self-identity of the person. A state of 'being', on the other hand, is one in which the person's identity and self-worth are based on the individual's own innate capacity to achieve a quality of life that is largely independent from one's standard of living. Achieving such a quality of life is characterised by a level of self-sufficiency, inner peace and the absence of a relentless pursuit of consumer goods.

Principles such as these had little bearing on the approach to development that emerged out of the Industrial Revolution. The factory was the dominant organisational model, and society applied this model to the management of people and of social problems. We need to change this to a commitment to holism – an approach to reality as an integrated whole, whose properties are more than the sum of its parts and cannot be reduced to those of smaller units.

The overriding task of this current generation is to rise above its experience of betrayal and to work towards a collective, conscious decision regarding the nature of its legacy to future generations – looking to development from a systemic, holistic perspective.

But to secure this legacy for future generations, new global frameworks are essential, said **Lorna Gold**, according to her research examining business and social responses to the adverse impacts of globalisation. World debates have been tackling many issues, such as chronic poverty, inequality, growing insecurity, environmental destruction and other factors:

Many of these debates and conferences have failed to address key concerns that will determine the future of millions of people in dire poverty on this planet. While many governments and individuals may have good ideas and strong values, somehow the sum of their efforts do not add up. The final outcome was almost inevitably a watered-down compromise with no real substance for change.

One of the critical factors is that the underlying 'neo-liberal model' has come to dominate the circles, making decisions in both the economic and political fields. In the absence of shared beliefs and values across the world, neo-liberal globalisation has become a de facto ethic in which the market decides who is valuable and who is worthless. We need to re-think how our economy relates to other aspects of life. We need to consider three arenas in which change can take place: in public policy making, in private institutions and at a 'person in community' level.

Change is needed at a public policy level. We need new models, new frameworks, fresh insights into policy. We need to re-frame economic policy in ways that make us think not only about our own self-interest but of global self-interest. This requires a radical change in perspective and an ability to think coherently about the overall unifying vision in which all other policies have to be placed. At the same time, humanising the global economy requires changes in private institutions. Most importantly, it requires a radical rethink of the role of business and civil society organisations, such as the rise in corporate social responsibility and civil society engaging in business. Finally, there is change at the individual and community level. We need to shift from life choices based solely on self-interest alone, to ones based on an ethic of responsibility.

So how do these three levels interlink? The linkages between them are crucial and highlight the need for a radically different vision that no longer sees economic life as somehow detached from the rest of life, immune from the normal ethical and moral responsibilities that we face in our daily lives. It requires us to see economic space as a space that is relational, involving myself and my relationship with others.

The seeds of a different economy are all around us. One positive example is the little-known movement called the Economy of Sharing. This grew in Brazil where many individuals were faced with the tragic effects of social injustice. This involved a group of business people applying their vision of unity to their organisations so as to create businesses that not only related to the community but were designed to give back and share with the poorest. This Economy of Sharing project has since grown internationally and is an example of how the business community, motivated by a strong ethical vision, can respond to the imperative of humanising the global economy.

'The seeds of a different economy are all around us'

This demonstrates that we urgently need to re-think our understanding of economic freedom. Our economic thinking has generally followed the freedom *from* perspective, seeing each individual as an isolated unit. This vision is no longer tenable.

We need a radical shift to a freedom *to* perspective. This is much more challenging, since freedom to do things and to be somebody means taking relationships with others seriously in economic life. This means reorienting our vision to put communion at the heart of what we do.

But this 'freedom to' can only be achieved in the context of civil society and wider governance structures, explained Concern's **David Begg**:

The big issue is about the reform of the corporate and institutional sector in the context of globalisation of the world economy. The shift in the balance of power towards these sectors caused by the globalisation phenomenon makes the existing order of control and governance non-viable in the longer term. Nation states must act to ensure that the governance structures of these bodies serve social interests and not just those of shareholders as happens in the existing corporate/financial nexus. The economic forces of globalisation are proceeding rapidly, while we have yet to get a handle on the social implications in a world that is very badly divided between rich and poor.

The vibrancy of civil society is a vital factor in this. Our democracy is about more than electing a government. It is about different interests in society combining to hold that government accountable, even though the same interests may be in tension with one another for much of the time. It is the totality of these relationships that makes up civil society.

'Our democracy is about more than electing a government'

Globalisation represents the comprehensive victory of capitalism over communism, but the diminution of social values has left us bereft of a global ethic with which to harness and control the forces of inequality released by this new economic order. Globalisation is a process of global economic integration broadly driven by market forces, in particular the competitive price pressures to reduce costs, but the actual events of industrial movements depend crucially upon political transactions. Concessions are offered, deals are made, investment follows.

Global integration of the consumer market also has a social dimension. With the breakdown of national boundaries in trade, communications and travel, people all over the world are becoming part of an integrated consumer market. But integration has been an uneven process. While the global elite are consumers in an integrated market, many others are marginalised out of the global consumption network.

Let us look at the role of the international institutions and governments in the global market. In terms of the forces at work, there are some key differences between the present situation and previous periods of instability in the world economy. In particular, the interaction between private sector behaviour, institutional structures and financial liberalisation has not been experienced before. Governments must seek to enforce a new model of global corporate governance in addition to reform of the institutions controlling the financial system. The responsibility to change from shareholder-driven corporate governance to one that includes much wider goals is primarily one for the governments of the major trading nations.

The history of industrial development has taught societies everywhere to think of the economic order as a ladder. Some people are high up the ladder. Others are struggling to climb it. The new dynamic of globalisation paints a different metaphor in people's minds – a see-saw – in which some people fall in order that others may rise. But people have to re-imagine an economic order based on different metaphors. Not a ladder or a see-saw. Perhaps a vast playground where many different children are playing together and separately, but all playing the same game.

There is a continuum between politics in its most basic form, in the way people engage in civil society, the governance institutions and corporations in the New World Order, and whether this New World Order is to be inclusive or to serve the consumer elite of the developed world only.

Engaging in such a New World Order implies collective responsibility, according to **Melanie Verwoerd**, then the South African Ambassador to Ireland:

None of us can deny that all is not well in this global village. We are increasingly faced with a world where, despite a tremendous increase in wealth and affluence in some parts, more and more people are faced with desperate and dehumanising poverty – making them feel like foreigners in this global village.

How do we address this? There is the global and the individual perspective. But in both cases the process starts with awareness – with listening. But listening is often not enough: we must also truly hear. In our world today we know more than ever before what is going on – we know about the poverty and the violence. None of us can claim ignorance. But through maybe self-protection or feelings of helplessness, we have succeeded in listening to these things without really hearing.

To start hearing, to listen deeply, we have to look each other in the eyes and understand this collective responsibility that we hold towards each other; to understand that we are responsible not only for ourselves or our families or even our society, but that we share a collective responsibility towards all those with whom we share this earth. Once we have come to hear the pain, we have to understand that the inequality and pain does not come about in a vacuum, but is created by, amongst others, current global systems and our lifestyles in the 'one-thirds world'. Clearly this means that at a national, international and individual level we need real change.

Experience from South Africa suggests that people do not like to be reminded of collective responsibilities. People are privatising their citizenship – and daily living becomes a never-ending rush or drive to maintain this privacy through material wealth. Even in Ireland it seems that increasing concerns are being raised about this gradual loss of community. It seems that this

'Listening is not enough: we must also truly hear' tendency to privatise citizenship is also mirrored in our global citizenship and a lack of consciousness about how our lives directly influence those of others. Thus, the developed world has the wealth and resources not because the developing world is hopeless or stupid, but because of global systems that mostly benefit the developed world.

But there is a further level of privatisation that urgently needs to be countered. This level of privatisation involves the natural world. Fundamentally it seems that the human race is increasingly claiming its right to take what we want (and not necessarily need) with very little regard for the effect this is having on the natural world and the environment. It seems that unless we can see ourselves as not only part of the human global order, but also responsible players in the natural global environment, we will eventually privatise ourselves into extinction.

However, properly grasped, globalisation can bring many benefits, according to **Tina Roche**. Roche, then chief executive of the Foundation for Investing in Communities, argued that globalisation is an inescapable fact of modern life, upon which, more than ever before, we are interdependent:

There are many detractors of globalisation and some people even think globalisation is the problem. The case has rightly been made that globalisation has been badly managed by the world authorities. Western countries like us are hypocritical; we want to compete in all markets, but we do not want others to compete in ours. We ask African countries to live by standards that we ourselves refuse to live by. Western countries gain disproportionate benefits at the expense of the developing world. Globalisation today is not working for many of the world's poor. It is not working for the environment, for economic stability or to lessen poverty.

But global capitalism has brought huge benefits. Just because it has been badly managed does not mean we should throw the baby out with the bath water. Mass markets have brought a range of quality goods and services within the reach of a far broader group of ordinary people. Open markets also mean an open forum for ideas.

There are things we can do as a people to address some of the challenges posed by globalisation. At its most basic level, businesses need to continue to provide for employment, because employment alleviates poverty and in most cases it is a pointer towards better prosperity. Companies should also ensure that as well as providing employment, their end products are safe for consumption. Occupation laws need to be embraced and people need to be trained to a high standard. Environmental concerns need to be tackled further. Sustainability needs to be the guiding principle on which decisions are taken. Gender balance must be a goal.

With a little effort we could have openness and transparency as a characteristic of business. Businesses should not hide mistakes, which many do at present. What does our responsible business look like? In relation to ecology and environment, the company should be formally committed to sustainable development. There should be a continuous striving for improvement in relation to the efficiency with which the company uses all forms of energy, recycling products, reducing carbon emissions. Priorities should also be for health and safety in the workplace, with diversity and empowerment among employees, meeting concerns about freedom of association and the right to engage in collective bargaining. The companies should establish formal mechanisms to maximise promotion in the communities in which they operate and the community should be seen as an important stakeholder.

In this way business could be seen as the solution to the world's problems and not the cause. Business could use their influence, unique capabilities and grassroots presence for widespread good. Globalisation is a fact of life and there is no going back. With interdependence there comes a need for collective action. Global companies will therefore need global governments. We should remember that corporate responsibility is really only personal responsibility collectivised.

'Global companies need global governments'

Effective response to globalisation is critical, according to **Eoin O'Driscoll**, then managing director of Aderra, who addressed the fundamental changes in the global business environment:

We need to understand and respond to those changes. Markets are becoming much more open; competition is more international and intense; technology is enabling global trading and new business models; the value chain is increasingly disaggregated, with activities distributed to their most economic or strategic location. Outsourcing, insourcing, offshoring and nearshoring are now part of our everyday lives. We are experiencing the 'McDonaldisation of society'.

Globalisation is now extending beyond goods to encompass services. Internationally-traded services are forming an increasingly important component of trade in the economies of the more developed countries and will be a growing source of high-skilled, knowledge-intensive jobs and a competitive advantage for the future. The growing importance of knowledge will be that individuals, companies and countries increasingly seek to differentiate themselves and build new sources of competitive advantage based on knowledge and expertise.

O'Driscoll reported at the time that the cost of doing business in Ireland had risen significantly. As a high-wage open economy we must deliver the productivity and differentiation in goods and services that will allow us to extract value from customers and markets as we compete globally:

The real challenge for all of us is recognising that the global environment is changing at a rapid pace and that we must respond to this avalanche of change as a matter of urgency. We know from evolution that it is not the strongest of the species that survive, or the most intelligent, but those most adaptive to change. As a country, we are too small to be slow. We cannot afford inertia. We must learn not only to survive change, but to predict it, get ahead of it, embrace it, thrive in it. This can and should be our real competitive advantage. This will require agility: agile minds, agile strategies and agile structures.

With continued globalisation the issue of values is even more pressing, as emphasised by **Philip Lowe**, then director general for competition at the European Commission. Lowe described how the banking crisis had highlighted the fundamental interconnection between what banks and other financial institutions do and what happens in the rest of the economy and society:

This has given rise to increasing calls for regulation of the financial sector. While improved regulation is obviously essential, we must also look beyond regulation to the systemic relationship between banks and the real economy. The key issue is that private companies and banks should on their own, as well as in the general interest, respect some public values and accept some civic responsibilities, going beyond compliance with regulation. Our societies and our economies comprise complex relationships of interdependence and interconnection, whether in markets or more widely in social networks. And these relationships depend for their effectiveness on trust and confidence between all those involved. As well as regulation, we need to look for some form of contractualisation between banks and the rest of society. There should be commitments to codes of best practice on lending to individuals and firms. There should be commitments to support growth and employment in the communities where banks are located. There must be, in the end, a recognition by the financial sector of some civic responsibilities that go along with the freedom they have to create value for their shareholders.

Powerlessness and Inequity: Taking Responsibility

Powerlessness corrupts by eroding the sense of personal responsibility that is central to any kind of ethical conduct. The feeling of being powerless to effect improvement in one's situation is a condition with which large numbers of people claim to be afflicted. The need to shift towards a more egalitarian society is even more pressing in the current context of globalisation. We have to take action, participate, engage. No one is powerless – power is present in every moment of every day, and in every relationship.

Whilst it is undoubtedly true that absolute power corrupts absolutely, we would also reverse that statement and it would be equally true, said *Irish Times* columnist **Fintan O'Toole** – we could also say that powerlessness corrupts and that absolute powerlessness corrupts absolutely:

Morality is based on one very fundamental human quality, which is the quality of choice. If you do not have a choice to make, you cannot make ethical decisions. The state of being without the capacity to make choices or decisions is powerlessness. Powerlessness corrupts by eroding the sense of personal responsibility that is central to any kind of ethical conduct. You lose the capacity to take responsibility for your actions.

What has all this to do with modern Ireland? In modern Ireland we know all about, or we should know all about, the corrupting effects of absolute powerlessness as well as corrupting effects of absolute power. We know what happens when power

'Powerlessness corrupts by eroding the sense of personal responsibility'

is not held accountable. Coinciding with the development of a certain kind of prosperity, we have a new awareness of corruption, a new awareness of the erosion of ethics, particularly in public life. It is probably true to say that both political and business life in Ireland up to the 1960s was more ethical in some respects than it is now. What you had in most of the history of this state were two very ethical restraints on the behaviour of people who had power in the economic sphere or in the political sphere. Those restraints were politics and faith. For most of the people who established this state, there was a genuine and fundamental sense of idealism.

By contrast, one of the forces that has operated to break this idealism down is the large process by which, for example, the word ideology has become a term of abuse in politics. We pushed ourselves in a direction of valuing a kind of pragmatism, a short-termism, a sense of getting things done, of immediate achievement. Also, the sense of religious obligation, which may have been driven by hypocrisy, was a very important restraint on people's activities. This also has very fundamentally eroded in Irish society.

Through these two things we have lost the restraints that were there on certain kinds of behaviour. The fundamental weakness of the old system of public ethics from which we have come is that it was imposed from the top down. It did not depend on people making choices but on people having no choice. But one way or another that kind of coercive morality was going to disappear as the society changed and the twentieth century moved on. One of the fundamental weaknesses of the system of public morality that we had was that it concentrated much more on the private sphere than on the public sphere.

If we are going to construct a new public morality, it is very important that we get the order in which things have happened right. It is not prosperity that has eroded ethics. It is the erosion of ethics that has determined the nature of our prosperity. The key period in the development of contemporary Irish society was the period between the late 1980s and the early 1990s. It was in that period that the question of who would have power and who would not have power was essentially decided. What is critical and tragic is that it was also the time at which the erosion of public ethics was at its most sharp, most appalling and most vulgar. We lost the restraints on the behaviour of people in power. The loss of any sense of ethical restraint on the part of very significant sections of Irish society was at its strongest. Very significant sections of the political and business elite withdrew their allegiance to the state.

The effect of that was to shape kinds of prosperity in which there would be winners and losers. The function of the corruption was to ensure first of all that in the very difficult process of social adjustment, those who were able to buy their way out of having to share the burden could do so.

Powerlessness or disempowerment is a predicament regularly ascribed to individuals or groups who complain of disadvantage or victimisation, said professor of history at NUI Galway, **Gearóid Ó Tuathaigh**. The feeling of being powerless to effect improvement in one's situation is a condition with which large numbers of people claim to be afflicted:

The abiding message from public discussion is one of powerlessness, although it is not necessarily unique to Ireland. The feeling of powerlessness that people are experiencing arises from several issues: globalisation – remoteness and inadequacy to grasp the logic of globalisation; diminishing role of community in our advanced society – isolation in the more advanced industrial society. In spite of all that, there have been significant developments, for example the efforts at addressing the issues of powerlessness, empowerment, exclusion and inclusion – especially social partnership, consultation, bottom-up development.

However, the declining level of popular participation in the voluntary and community sector is itself a problem. The mobilisation of communities for collective political purposes seems to be increasingly reactive in character, responding to decisions already made by the authorities. What is missing in many communities is a rooted and coherent sense of collective responsibility and capacity for building their own community, a coherent vision and comfortably shared vision of themselves as a community. It is in this vital area of vision, values and vocabulary (the language of empowerment) that the main challenge of the coming decade may be found. The most challenging project facing community leaders in the coming decade will be the creation of a new inspiring language and social vision that goes beyond economic growth as an end in itself. This involves the paradigm of right relationships, informed by global ethical and environmental considerations. This is a demand for a new social vision and an answer to the question, 'What kind of society do we want to be?'

'What is missing in many communities is a rooted and coherent sense of collective responsibility'

We should not underestimate the challenge to create a new language of social vision that is grounded in reality and in achievable goals informed by worthy and humane values.

The economic or material base of our living is a critical element. But we need to find a vision of society that subsumes the economic base, that is humane and socially integrating. It will need to have a strong emancipatory edge, to be liberationist in tone, and its convictions will need to be carried into practice to empower people, living as members of multiple interlocking communities (family, neighbourhood, city, county, region, global), to empower people in these complex and interlocking relationships so that they can have a meaningful sense of human agency, in shaping their lives and in developing the environment and communities in which they live.

This need to shift towards a more egalitarian society is even more pressing in the current context of globalisation, according to founder member of the Equality Studies Centre at UCD **Kathleen Lynch**:

A very small number of transnational corporations either own or control vast amounts of the world's wealth. The interests of global capital dictate the progress of the global economy. To create new social institutions and new political structures that will ensure that global economic developments serve the interest of those without capital, it is imperative that we invest time and energy in developing new ideas about society and its social and political institutions.

> '*A very small number of transnational corporations either own or control vast amounts of the world's wealth*'

At present, many of the great achievements of western civilisation are being threatened by the rise of the New Right. Economic monetarism has become a type of religion; increasingly, the only work that is of value is that which can be exchanged for profit. By logical extension, those who are unable to be economically productive or profit generating are deemed valueless; they are degraded and marginalised.

There are three core equality issues that must be addressed in the pursuit of a socially just society. The first of these is the issue of economic equality (fundamentally an issue of the distribution – including ownership and control – and redistribution of primary goods); the second is socio-cultural and symbolic equality (fundamentally an issue of the recognition and respect for differences); and the third is political equality (fundamentally an issue of parity in the representation of interests). These equality issues have their origins in distinct forms of injustice that exist in society, namely economic injustices, political and civil injustices and socio-cultural and symbolic injustices.

If we are to create a new vision for Ireland, a realisable vision, then we must begin to challenge the ideologies of neo-liberalism, dressed up as it is in the fatalistic clothes of 'globalisation' and 'flexible' labour markets. We must identify the principles and procedures that will guide our social, economic and political institutions through systematic research, analysis and planning. While life cannot be made to order, the quality of our life can be greatly improved by collaborative work between all those with an interest in creating a caring, participative and socially just society.

There are three core contexts in which we need to work actively to create an egalitarian society, namely the economic context, the political context and the socio-cultural context. These are the three basic equality principles that need to guide action in each of these if we are to have a socially just society – we need more effective and fairer mechanisms for the redistribution of wealth; we need to put operational procedures throughout all our cultural institutions that recognise and celebrate differences; and we need to develop systems for the representation of interests in power and decision-making that are effectively, as opposed to formally, inclusive.

Everything is linked, explained **Paula Downey** of Downey Youell Associates:

We live and work in a system of power that is real, the net effect of which is to keep us economically productive and politically docile and limited in our sense of what it is we are here to do. This system operates with our collusion, it is only kept in place by our willingness to buy its message, to believe.

We will engage more effectively in bringing about change if we take a systems view of how things happen: the ecology

> **'Power shapes our world and we need to understand the more prevalent kinds of power we experience'**

of change. Complex systems are not 'made', they are self-making and no one is in charge. Complex systems make themselves; the system brings itself to life as the components of the system help to make each other. Systems make themselves by taking information from the environment and responding to it. Information is the key ingredient in life because information organises life, or helps life to self-organise, and new information helps living systems to evolve.

There is an important dimension of social systems we must pay attention to if we are interested in changing things, and that is power. Power shapes our world and we need to understand the more prevalent kinds of power we experience, working from the obvious to the more subtle and very potent forms of power.

Power 1 is the power of veto, about who wins in decision-making, who has power over whom and who can get someone to do something they might not otherwise do. This is obvious, observable power – employers, unions, winners and losers in conflict. Power 2 is the power that prevents conflict from emerging at all, the power that controls what is discussed and what is not discussed, the power to influence the agenda, manipulation and hidden coercion – government, big business and media do it all the time. Power 3 controls the entire system by controlling the ideas and relationships that shape the system itself. This is about influencing what people want and what they do not want. Thus, the real power of society lies with those that determine the basic framing ideas of our society: goals and values. Powers 1, 2 and 3 are about power over other people but Power 4 is about power with people. This is the power that springs up whenever people get together and act together. While 'power over' is about descendent power – coming from the top – 'power with' is ascendant power that percolates from people right throughout the system, and that is what utterly transforms the system. Power

5 is an extension of this – power *within*. We have to take action, participate, engage; no one is powerless, power is present in every moment of every day and in every relationship.

Power *within* is the fuel of the engine of power *with*. Each of us has power, so we also have responsibility – not just for the here and now, but for all the visible repercussions down the line. Power over, the power dynamic we are inside, keeps things the same ... but only so long as we do not see its hold on us. Power with and power within have the potential to change the world.

The Role of the Media: Consumerism and Self-Interest

What is the role of the media in relation to popular culture, asked writer and journalist **Tom McGurk**. What is popular culture and what is it that culture seeks to popularise?

Consumerism is now beginning to represent itself in pernicious ways in the media. So we arrive at the concept of the message, both liminal and subliminal. This has been so effective for advertising that now it has passed into politics and into democratic society. This is the route of tabloidism.

Where is the sovereignty of the fact? Information is the oxygen of democracy. Is it not underscored by critical analysis, veracity, socio-economic subtext, but instead is a series of facts in quotes, chosen by the rules of product placement, in thrall not to the demands of objective analysis but to the requirements of consumerism. In other words, have facts and information become products to sell? Where does all this leave the conduct of public affairs by the media in a democratic society? Tabloidism very quickly builds its own constituency.

'Information is the oxygen of democracy'

In Ireland, a new tabloid generation is emerging, principally the younger generation located in working-class areas. These people no longer have the protection of association with the great defining things of Irish life – extended family, sense of place, parish, community, church. These are people who live between different wants of consumerism. Have we reached the stage where freedom of speech has the right to enslave itself?

We are facing a crisis of identity. As the new consumerism and media age that lies just ahead of us masses its forces, and as the people who control the spread of news and information in our society, and the people who own the consumerist empires, become one and the same people, we face a potentially extraordinary society. We used to joke that our job as journalists was merely filling in the spaces between the advertisements. This is no longer a joke. It is becoming increasingly the case. We find that the people who own the goods that they are flogging during the commercial breaks are also the people who own the programming that is broadcast between those commercial breaks. The emperors of the new television age seek the imprimatur of caring and goodness for their commercial intentions.

Editorial then ceases to be independent and sovereign in its own context. Instead it is becoming yet another weapon in the consumerist's armoury. This produces light entertainment programmes that are just verbal chewing gum and serves to stunt all types of development. But there has also been a growth of non-fictional programmes that represents a serious threat to journalism and to how democratic society sees itself.

This is the business of attempting to popularise fact. Crime programming, human relations programmes and news programmes have become low-life showbiz, not as a show of concern for society but a source of entertainment. Crime programmes intrude on personal lives without asking real questions about crime. Human relations programmes intrude on family relationships and personal difficulties. News programmes are often about mere gossip. This is information entertainment, or 'info-tainment'.

Journalists are the hewers of information and carriers of fact. A hack is a labourer at the bottom of the democratic heap. In the triumvirate of society, the hack is the man who supplies the punter with the information in the ballot box, in deciding against which politician they will put their X. The hack should have no axe to grind, either on behalf of consumerism or popularity. In fact, he should always say the unpopular thing and always ask the unpopular question.

This self-interest of the media was also highlighted by writer and journalist **John Waters**, who argued that one of the reasons we do not understand or look too closely at the media is that there is no conduit of any kind for discussion of the media other than the media themselves:

First of all, the media have a special interest in preventing too close a scrutiny of how they operate. Media examine and interrogate all other elements of society, but the one element of society that is beyond scrutiny to a very high degree is the media themselves. There is within professional journalism a disingenuousness about this, a persistent assertion that absolute freedom, or something close to absolute freedom, exists, that media represent reality as it is and that there is no background noise, no contamination. That is a completely false proposition and it misleads people who are not in a position to examine the media. There is a very different way, a very subtle way in which media operate. Many subtle and deceptive surfaces are created.

> 'The media have a special interest in preventing too close a scrutiny of how they operate'

These deceptive surfaces are created by the promotion of assumptions and attitudes that conform to the media view, the suppression of dissent by moral pressure and the loss of alternative viewpoints by the 'clubability' of the profession of journalism.

As a result, the idea that what we read in the newspapers is some kind of representation of spontaneous reality is complete fiction. It is an ideological presentation of reality, a partial presentation, which emerges in quite a sophisticated and very subtle and complex way. There is a spontaneous cultural collusion that feeds off all kinds of interests, fears, prejudices, desires, ambitions, and all these converge to create what you see on the front page in the morning. What's on the front page is not – objectively speaking – the important things that happened yesterday. What is on the front page is what a certain group of people, coming from a certain kind of cultural and ideological and professional background, thought was important enough to present to you of what happened yesterday.

For the future of the media, there needs to be a human perspective, a degree of self-scrutiny, a criticism that does not exist at the moment and a genuine opening up of real freedom of expression.

Echoing these concerns, communications lecturer **Colum Kenny** spoke of how the relationship between citizens and the media needs to be redefined urgently:

This is not least because so much of our experience is filtered through the media. It is a process that begs questions about control and ownership and about the manner in which the media influences our identity as individuals or as a society. Because the media is so pervasive, we need to deepen our understanding of its complexity.

The media has increasingly become culture for many people. If an event is not on the papers, or on the radio, TV or worldwide web, then to all intents and purposes it has not happened for the public. The media shapes our agenda, indicating to us what matters and, by its omission, what does not. What people discuss is so often what is discussed by the media. Politics, art, fashion – formative opinions on these and on other aspects of our cultural life reach most people through the media. This is not necessarily a bad thing, but it does illustrate the potential

'The media shapes our agenda'

power of media. Illustrating this is the fact that the structures and values of the media itself form part of the message received consciously or unconsciously by the public. These include an internal relationship of power between proprietor and employees and the increasing adoption of consumerist or marketing criteria.

There are challenges around the growth in mass media consumption. Deregulation and increased competition, coupled with the sophisticated targeting of particular markets, as well as the 'branding' of products, are creating a landscape in which, for many citizens, the media not only constitutes their culture but sets the agenda for what they regard as desirable, important or even realistic.

The media's dependence on advertising and niche marketing has led to what we can call 'consumer totalitarianism', reflecting the ideology of our consumerist society. This is justified by its proponents as giving people what they want, as if indulging material attachments or fantasies was somehow a moral virtue or socially desirable. Like the feeding of any habit, it is also stimulating greater attachment to, and fantasies regarding, consumerism.

For example, stimulation by the media is crucial in the process of attracting audiences, and one of the prime functions of media stimulation is the creation of an environment in which people are responsive to the sales messages of advertisers. This dependence on advertising means that media managers are disinclined to bite the commercial hand that feeds them by challenging forcefully the interest or ideology of the dominant groups that provide their investment or revenues. As a result, where broadcasting was once seen as a means of informing, educating and entertaining, it is now seen increasingly as a way of entertaining and selling.

> **'Dependence on advertising means that media managers are disinclined to bite the commercial hand that feeds them'**

For all these reasons it is crucial that citizens take a more active interest in the matter of who controls the media, who monitors the media, what the media actually says or implies and how the media creates and reinforces people's opinions, identity and value systems.

In taking this interest, citizens need healthy cynicism and personal values, according to political commentator **Denis Bradley**, who highlighted how, within a hundred years, the media has changed radically:

Some might maintain that the media is only interested in sleaze and bad news. The reality is that the media is one of our most valuable tools of communication. It is as much an expression of who we are as are our politics, our churches, our health services or our transport systems. At its best, it is the eyes and ears of a people, providing insight into the other powerful institutions of the state. But the media is also a business, available to us because of the dynamics of economics and influenced by the vagaries of economics, just as most other aspects of life are. Whether it has enough space for good news is a moot point.

Some will argue that it has to be recognised that we live in a time of much materialism and commercialism, of low values and elastic ethics. Some will claim that much of this state of affairs is due to an undue influence and penetration of an unrestricted and intrusive media. This particular view is that an unethical and value-free media has become so pervasive and influential that it has corrupted much of life and destroyed values and traditions that have served society well. This viewpoint would say that those values and traditions are given scant attention and little space in the media and thus there is little or no room for good news stories.

But helpful here is the healthy cynicism in our psyche and personality, also possibly existing in our culture. This is a trait that is cynical and at times mocking of the frailty and fallibility of all institutions, particularly when those institutions become overly precious or inflated with their own importance. This is a trait that acknowledges the necessity of institutions while at the same time recognises that the human spirit cannot be constrained or restrained within the confines of any or all institutions. This healthy cynicism does not stop with institutions. It is perhaps more scathing or mocking of individuals who are full of their own self-importance and who seek to inflate their status and influence.

This trait, if we have lost it, needs to be re-established and exercised. It is helpful and healthy when dealing with any institution, and is vital when dealing with the media. In this age, aspects of the media relish celebrity and fame. It is obsessed with money, beauty and status. That aspect of the media is prone to insert itself into the story. It desires to be part of the status, the money and the beauty. It is self-serving and self-centred. The only healthy response to that world is a healthy dose of sarcasm and mockery, and it is even more healthy when some of that mockery is turned on oneself. The media will always be subject to the men and women who are its readers, its listener and its viewers. If those men and women are creating good stories for themselves within their communities and those same people see the media as a way of telling those stories to other people then there will always be ample room in the media for good news.

When we accept and value our own self we cease to be afraid of other people. We no longer have superiors and inferiors, only equals with whom we can co-operate and share while we take responsibility for ourselves. We no longer feel deprived and envious, so we can abandon revenge and greed. Because we value ourselves, we value others. We reject those who try to dominate and manipulate us. If we all decided to

> '*The only healthy response to the world of the media is a healthy dose of sarcasm and mockery*'

accept and value ourselves, we would cause those who have power over us a great deal of trouble.

Conclusion

Much of the power and leadership debate has been around the concept of leadership of service, focusing on truth and integrity. Visions should develop and change, supported by strategic leadership. Organisations must focus on longer-term quality. Coping with globalisation, combating powerlessness and the role of the media have been central challenges. Coupled with the related issues of social capital and resourcing people, this presents a demanding agenda in the search for future directions.

Contributors

Are We Forgetting Something?
Edited by Harry Bohan and
Gerard Kennedy
(Veritas Publications, 1999)

Chair
Marie Martin, John Quinn,
Michael Kenny

A Soul for Society
Sr Therese, Poor Clare Convent,
Ennis

Climbing Into Our Proper Dark
Mark Patrick Hederman,
Glenstal Abbey

Soulless Society
John Lonergan, governor of
Mountjoy Prison

A Sense of Place
Professor J. J. Lee, Department
of History at University College
Cork

Towards a New Ireland
Tom McGurk, columnist and
broadcaster

From Boom to Bust and Back
David McWilliams, economist
and writer

Is it Possible to Manage the
Future?
John Drew, Durham University
Business School

One World – Ready or Not
David Begg, Concern

Social Entrepreneurship
Mary Redmond, solicitor

Working Towards Balance
Edited by Harry Bohan and
Gerard Kennedy
(Veritas Publications, 2000)

Chair
Marian Harkin

Does Power Erode Ethics?
Fintan O'Toole, journalist

The Human Dimension in the
Workplace
Catherine McGeachy, Vision
Consultants

Corporate Responsibility to
Communities
Stephen Covey, Franklin Covey
Company

The Challenges of Success
Tom Collins, NUI Maynooth

Love and Work in the Millennium
Miriam Moore, clinical psychologist

The Growth Illusion
Richard Douthwaite, writer

Is Balance a Myth?
John O'Donohue, poet and philosopher

Redefining Roles and Relationships
Edited by Harry Bohan and Gerard Kennedy
(Veritas Publications, 2001)

Chair
David McWilliams

Contemplating Alternative Relationships of Power
Professor Gearóid O Tuathaigh, NUI Galway

Rebuilding Social Capital
Maureen Gaffney, psychologist and writer

Rise of Science, Rise of Atheism
Professor Bill Collins, Samford University, Alabama

Social Justice and Equality in Ireland
Kathleen Lynch, Equality Studies Centre of UCD

Diversity Practices at Hewlitt Packard
Orla Kelly, Hewlitt Packard

Business is a Means, Not an End
John Liddy, Roche Ireland

Putting People at the Centre of Things
Robert Lane, Yale University

Why Are We Deaf to the Cry of the Earth?
Fr Seán McDonagh, Columban Missions

Its Just the Media
Colum Kenny, Dublin City University

Is the Future My Responsibility?
Edited by Harry Bohan and Gerard Kennedy
(Veritas Publications, 2002)

Chair
Doireann Ní Bhriain

The New World of Elephants and Fleas
Charles Handy, writer and broadcaster

Working With Change
Anne Coughlan, Irish Business and Employers Confederation

Civic Expression – The Value of Volunteering
Freda Donoghue, School of Business Studies, Trinity College Dublin

In Each Other's Shadow
Tom Healy, Department of Education and Science

Contributors

Taking Responsibility in a Changing World
Ged Pierse, Pierse Contracting

Systems and Power – Exploring the Ecology of Change
Paula Downey, Downey Youell Associates

Local Vision for Change – How Can We Do Things Differently?
Pádraig Ó Céidigh, Aer Arann

Global Vision for Change
Jim Power, economist, Friends First

Imagining the Future
Edited by Harry Bohan and Gerard Kennedy
(Veritas Publications, 2005)

Chair
John Quinn

Imagining the Future for Our Young People
Mike Cooley, writer and researcher

Imagining the Future in a Socially Responsible Business World
Tina Roche, Foundation for Investing in Communities

Imagining the Future of Our Schools
Catherine Byrne, Irish National Teachers' Organisation (INTO)

Imagining the Future for Organised Religion
Diarmuid Martin, Archbishop of Dublin

Imagining the Future – An Irish Perspective
Emily O'Reilly, Ombudsman

Imagining the Future – A Global Perspective
Michael D. Higgins, NUI Galway

Filling the Vacuum?
Edited by Harry Bohan
(Veritas Publications, 2006)

Chair
Rachael English

Counting on Community
Mary McAleese, President of Ireland

Employment in the Future: How Globalisation Will Impact Our Working Lives
Eoin O'Driscoll, chairman of Forfas

Prophets or Profits – Who Fills the Vacuum?
Marie Murray, psychologist and writer

What Value Do We Place on Sport?
Pat Duffy, Sports Coach UK

Responding to Spiritual Hunger
Peter McVerry SJ, worker with young people

The Media – Is There a Place for Good News?
Denis Bradley, political commentator

Living Scenes – Intergenerational Learning
Mary Surlis, NUI Galway

Freedom: Licence or Liberty?
Edited by Harry Bohan
(Veritas Publications, 2007)

Chair
Rachael English

The Best of Times, the Worst of Times
Finola Kennedy, economist, UCD

What We Have is What We Want
Janet Murray, Tivoli Institute for training in psychotherapy

Crime in Ireland
Paul Reynolds, crime correspondent for RTÉ

The Price of the Freedom Agenda
David Quinn, religious and social affairs commentator

Wasting Time with People
Alice Leahy, writer and broadcaster

Knowledge is Freedom, Freedom is Knowledge
John Quinn, producer with RTÉ

Tax and Community
Frank Daly, chairman of the Revenue Commissioners

Together We're Better
Mary Davis, Special Olympics Ireland

Tracking the Tiger: A Decade of Change
Edited by Harry Bohan
(Veritas Publications, 2008)

Chair
Rachael English

'Rich is Better'
Paul Tansey, economic consultant and journalist

The Myth of Free Speech
John Waters, journalist and author

Reflections on our Health Service
Maurice Neligan, cardiac surgeon

Religion and the Secular in Contemporary Ireland
Donal Murray, Bishop of Limerick

From Institution to Community
Mary Kealy, Brothers of Charity, Co. Clare

Searching for Foundation in Today's Society
Sean Love, Amnesty International

Policing – The Future
Kathleen O'Toole, Chief
Inspector of the Garda
Síochána Inspectorate

Delivering Justice – Enabling
Society
Nuala O'Loan, former Police
Ombudsman for Northern
Ireland

Family Life Today: The Greatest
Revolution?
Edited by Harry Bohan
(Veritas Publications, 2009)

Chair
Rachael English

The Family as the Foundation
of Society
Cardinal Seán Brady,
Archbishop of Armagh and
Primate of All Ireland

Family Well-Being
Kieran McKeown, social and
economic research consultant

Nomads – Will They Change
the Family?
Charles Handy, writer,
broadcaster and lecturer

A New Vision for the Changing
Family
John Yzaguirre, psychologist
and author

Implications of the New
Economic Reality for Economic
Life
Jim Power, economist, Friends
First

The Family in Irish Law
Geoffrey Shannon, solicitor and
lecturer in family law

Changing Family Patterns:
Altruism as the Greatest
Revolution
Marie Murray, psychologist and
writer

Home and School
Mary Forde, principal,
Presentation College, Athenry,
Co. Galway

Who's in Charge? Towards a
Leadership of Service
Edited by Harry Bohan
(Veritas Publications, 2010)

Chair
Rachael English and Cathy
O'Halloran

Private Enterprise,
Public Values and Civic
Responsibilities
Philip Lowe, European
Commission

Who's Minding the House?
Jim Power, economist, Friends
First

Re-imagining Community
Professor Ray Kinsella and
Maurice Kinsella (UCD)

**Spirituality and Environment –
Seeking a New Vision**
Michael Rodgers, Tearmann
Centre, Glendalough

**The Cultural Challenge – A
Living Systems Perspective**
Paula Downey, Downey Youell
Associates

**When the Well Runs Dry,
Where Do We Go From Here?**
Fr Michael Drumm, writer on
theology

**Re-imagining Political
Leadership**
Dearbhail McDonald, legal
editor of the *Irish Independent*